Good Writing Made Simple

Third Edition

Monique Ferrell

Julian Williams

New York City College of Technology
City University of New York (CUNY)

Kendall Hunt
publishing company

Cover image © Shutterstock, Inc.

www.kendallhunt.com
Send all inquiries to:
4050 Westmark Drive
Dubuque, IA 52004-1840

Copyright © 2008, 2012, 2015 by Kendall Hunt Publishing Company

ISBN 978-1-4652-6783-2

Printed in the United States of America

Contents

1 2 3 4 5

Words

Words are power. If you—as a reader, writer, or researcher—become skilled enough to use them effectively, the world is yours. Undeniably, words convey almost everything about the human experience: our wants, thoughts, feelings, passions, likes and dislikes, ideas, and meaning. As such, gaining a focused and precise use of words makes communicating with others easier and the outcome of human interaction meaningful.

As student writers, you will be asked to conduct research, analyze and interpret the writing of others, and express yourself both scholarly and creatively. Additionally, you will be expected to communicate with your professors and peers, and, when the time comes, you may be asked to use your writing as a means of communicating with the professional world. Whatever you are asked to do as a student writer, you must use the world of words to your advantage.

In order to accomplish this, you must first comprehend how words work. Essentially, you must understand that all words have a purpose or job: **diction** (the choice of the right words for the given context), **syntax** (the effective connection of chosen words), and **punctuation** (arranging words correctly to convey meaning).

audience: knowing what to say and how to say it

We all use coded speech. Instinctively, we know that we cannot use the same tone or set of words with everyone. We may have one kind of vocabulary for our parents or guardians and another for our friends. Similarly, we understand that we have a vocabulary for the workplace and another for our intimate relationships. The same rules apply when

1

writing as a student. We must learn what to say, when to say it, and how best to say it.

Here are some examples:

A text to a friend: What up son? Yo' hit me back when you decide what's cracking. Last nite was cray. Holla back.

A note to your parents: Gone out to hang—maybe the mall. C U later—Me :)

An email to a college professor:

Dr. Stokes,

If possible, I would like to meet with you to discuss my midterm grade. I am concerned about how I am doing in the course. I am unable to make your office hours, so I am hoping to schedule an appointment with you. Please email a list of dates and times that work best.

Thank You,

Paris James, English 1101 (Mon/Wed 11:30)

–NOT–

Hey Dr. S,

What happened with my midterm? I need an A in this class. Let's meet, okay?

P

—ɱ—

More often than not as a student writer, you will use the essay format to communicate ideas and feelings. As such, each time you write, you must be clear, concise, and reader-friendly. As a child, you first learned to master the simple sentence; it allowed you to obtain what you wanted and to express your visceral emotions: I want this; that is mine; give me that.

As student writers now in possession of an elevated vocabulary and a new understanding of how words work, you must set about using words to better articulate how you feel about something, someone, or a particular idea or subject.

Let's look at the following sentence:

The story was funny.

Technically, there is nothing wrong with this sentence, **BUT** it is flat and lacks details. Because it lacks specificity, the reader is left with more questions than information. Academic writing requires you to be much more specific, and it also requires that your writing be interesting and informative; in short, your reader should want to keep reading.

Let's try this instead:

Using humor and satire, Mohammed Naseehu Ali's "Mallim Sile" explores the topics of adult bullying and the use of faith as self-protection.

Here, the reader receives much needed additional information:
- The title of the story
- The author's name
- The subject matter or themes
- How and why the humor is used; as such, the word "funny" is now given a deeper meaning—a new and more informative context.

RESULT:

In order to find out how a story by this specific author about something as serious as adult bullying can be addressed with humor, the reader will now be more invested in discovering if they agree with your assessment.

building your vocabulary

English has the largest vocabulary of any language. So use it. You should, therefore, build up your word bank by regularly consulting a dictionary and thesaurus. If, for example, you look up the adjective "good" in a dictionary, some of the definitions you will find include "pleasant," "untainted," "kind," and "well-behaved." In a thesaurus, you will find "choice," "commendable," and "marvelous," among other synonyms. For antonyms, you will find "disagreeable," "naughty," and "worthless." While related to the word "good," all of these words have distinct meanings and should be chosen carefully.

To build up your vocabulary, we strongly recommend *Webster's New World Pocket Dictionary* as well as *Webster's New World Pocket Vocabulary*; both are inexpensive, palm-sized books designed for the college student. Nowadays, dictionary and thesaurus applications can also be easily downloaded to most cellular devices.

FYI

In many cases, colleges and universities have their own grammar websites that may appear on their writing center webpage. Examples of these grammar websites include the **CUNY WRITESITE** and the **Purdue University Writing Lab**. Also consider signing-up for the website **www.dictionary.com**, which will email you a "word of the day." The best way to build a vocabulary, enhance comprehension, and improve communication skills is, of course, to read extensively and frequently.

denotation and connotation

Although some words are very close in meaning, no two are exactly alike. The dictionary definition of a word is called the **denotation**. The **connotation** is a series of qualities, contexts, and emotional responses that the writer wants to associate with the implied meaning of a word. Take the word **apartheid**. The **denotation** is straight forward: a political and economic policy of segregation by race. The **connotation** of this word is wider: oppression, slavery, and inequality in a variety of contexts.

Compare, for example, the **denotation** and **connotation** of the word "bad" in the following sentences:

In 1976, The Buccaneers football team, with a record of 0-14, was really bad.

The denotation of "bad" here implies that the Buccaneers had a horrible season.

The 1985 Bears, who only lost one game all season, were a bad football team.

The connotation of "bad" here implies that the Bears were a great football team.

The precise **meaning** of any word is the sum of its denotation and its implied connotations. A writer aiming to communicate precisely will therefore choose words whose denotations are concrete and specific, and whose connotations fit the context.

two words or one?

When two or more small words appear together frequently, eventually they may become one word, sometimes with a different meaning. At any given moment in history, some paired words are written separately (*ice cream, may not*), some are hyphenated (*self-respect*) or contracted (*can't*), and some have already become one word (*everything, nothing, nevertheless, inasmuch as*).

Here are some of the pairs that are currently troublesome:

Ahold, A hold: As a singular term, "Ahold" is still seen as informal and may be viewed as bad form. The use of the word, however, is more commonly used these days. When used, it is often paired with the verb "get" and the preposition "of." "A hold" generally refers to the noun "hold" with the article "a."

*I grabbed **ahold** of his arm.*

*Get **ahold** of yourself.*

*During the tug of war match, I had **a hold** of the rope.*

All ready, already:

All ready (indefinite pronoun + adjective) means that everybody or everything is prepared. *Already* (adverb) means *at this time.*

*We are **all ready** for spring break.*

*I'm **already** thinking of spring break.*

All right: Always write as two words instead of "alright."

*Is it **all right** if we go shopping?*

Allot, a lot: As a single word, it means to parcel out. "A lot" means many or much.

*The school will **allot** each of us a computer.*

*This is **a lot** of work.*

Note: Alot is NOT a word.

All together, altogether: As two words, it means collectively. As a single word, it means entirely.

*We are traveling **all together** next month.*

*We are **altogether** too exhausted to continue.*

Along, a long: As a single word, it means over the length of; a line or course parallel and close to. "A long" is a measure of time or distance.

*I like to walk **along** the river bank.*

*Getting a degree takes **a long** time.*

Any more, anymore: "Anymore" and "Any more" are interchangeable. As a singular term, "anymore" may be seen as less formal. However, in English, "anymore" is a common adverb that is used in the negative sense

*I don't eat pork **anymore**.*

*I will never buy **anymore** printed books because I can't find **any more** book stores.*

*I don't go there **any more**.*

A part (noun), **apart** (adjective): "A part" refers to a piece of something that forms the whole of something. As a singular term, it means separated by distance or time; into pieces; separately.

*We all want **a part** of the American dream.*

*The loving couple is rarely **apart**.*

A while, awhile: "A while" is a noun meaning a length of time. "Awhile" is an adverb meaning for a time.

*Jensen slept for **a while**.*

*Jensen slept **awhile** before going to dinner.*

Everybody: always one word

***Everybody** is here.*

Everyday, every day: "Everyday" is an adjective that means daily or ordinary/common place. "Every day" is the same as "each day." Here, the adjective modifies the noun day.

***Every day**, you eat dinner.*

*You wash your face **every day**.*

*The trend is to use **everyday** recipes in the kitchen.*

Every one (adj. + pronoun), **everyone** (pronoun):

***Every one** of the students in this room is guilty of something.*

***Everyone** needs to confess.*

In fact: always two words

***In fact**, I do own a dog.*

In to, into: "In to" is the adverb "in" followed by the preposition "to." The main use of the preposition "into" is to indicate movement toward the inside of a place.

*The police wouldn't give **in to** the demands of the kidnappers.*

*Toni jumped **into** the lake.*

No one: Always write as two words instead of "noone."

*When Francisco called, **no one** answered the phone.* ˌ

Nevertheless: Always one word that means in spite of; notwithstanding.

*I am hungry; **nevertheless**, I am going directly to bed.*

Some day, someday: As two words, it refers to a single day—even if that day is unknown. As one word, it functions as an adverb that describes an indefinite future time.

*I have a doctor's appointment **some day** next month.*

*I'd like to me her again **someday**.*

Some time (adj. + noun), **sometimes** (adverb):

*I need **some time** to think.*

Sometimes, I feel like dancing.

Whereas: Always one word that means in contrast or in comparison to.

Whereas I have been a model student, I expect to graduate as valedictorian.

words that have more than one spelling

Adviser, advisor: *Adviser* is the preferred spelling, but *advisor* is frequently used and is not actually incorrect.

Aesthetic, esthetic: *Ae-* is the preferred spelling, but either is acceptable.

Altar, alter: *-ar* means a pedestal for prayer or meditation. *–er* means to change.

Allowed, aloud: *Allowed* means gave permission to. *Aloud* means spoken or said out loud.

Among, amongst: The *-st* extension is widely considered unnecessary. The same rule speaks to similar words like **while/whilst** and **amid/amidst**.

Ax, axe: *Ax* is the preferred spelling.

Backward, backwards: Both are correct, but when using the word as an adverb, *backward* is standard in American English and *backwards* is standard in British English.

Barbecue, barbeque: *Barbeque* is a variant of *barbecue* that comes from the truncation BBQ. Both are generally acceptable. When using one, remain consistent throughout.

Canceled, cancelled: In American English, the verb *cancel* is usually inflected *canceled* and *canceling* with one l. This is not the rule in Canadian, British, and Australian English, where the *-ll* is more common. Either spelling is generally accepted.

Collectable, collectible: *-ible* is the preferred variant.

Disc, disk: *Disc* is a variant of *disk*. However, *-sc* has become very common when referring to music and computers and similar media.

Donut, doughnut: *Donut* is an informal variant of *doughnut*. However, both are commonly accepted spellings.

Enquire, inquire: *Inquire* is the preferred American English spelling, and *E-* is the common British spelling. However, many use *enquire* in the sense of ask: *I **enquired** about her health. Inquire* is a formal investigation: *We are going to **inquire** into the accident.*

Flier, flyer: Outside the U.S. there is no difference. But in the U.S., pilots and passengers are *fliers,* and a posted paper is a *flyer.*

Fulfill, fulfil: *-ll* is the common American spelling. *-l* is preferred spelling outside of North America. **Note:** the spelling preferences extend to *fulfilment* and *fulfillment,* but not *fulfilled, fulfilling,* and *fulfiller,* which always have two l's.

Inflamed, enflamed: To arouse passionate feeling or action. *En-* is a variant of *inflamed.*

Nite, night: *Nite* is an informal variant of *night.* The first spelling is considered extremely casual and would be incorrect in standard writing.

Okay, Ok, o.k.: All three mean acceptable, passable, or good. All are acceptable forms of the word. When using one, be consistent throughout your writing.

Regardless, irregardless: The *ir-* is commonly used in dialectical American speech, but it is generally thought to be bad form. Avoid and use *regardless.*

Theater, theatre: Both are acceptable, but *theater* is more common.

Toward, towards: In American English, *towards* is an informal variant of *toward.* The -s is often a result of regional speaking voice. In standard writing, there is no -s. **Upward, upwards** follows the same explanation.

troublesome words and homophones

FYI

A homophone is a word that is pronounced the same as another word but differs in meaning, and may differ in spelling.

A, an, the: The definite article (*the*) and the indefinite article (*a* or *an*) are a sub-category of the adjective. Which indefinite article to use depends on the sound, not the spelling, of the word that follows.

Before words beginning with a consonant sound, use *a*:

a boat

a hospital

a union

Before words beginning with a vowel sound, use *an*:

an *apple*

an *eye*

an *hour*

Use *the* rather than *a* or *an* when referring to one or more specific items.
Grab **the** *bottle on your right.*

Use *a* or *an* rather than *the* when referring to something non-specific.
Grab **a** *bottle from the refrigerator.*

Accept, except: *Accept* is a verb meaning *to agree to take. Except* is a preposition meaning *excluding* or *but.*
Everyone **accepted** *the way things were* **except** *me.*

Advice, advise: *Advice* is a noun; *advise* is a verb.
The doctor knows how to **advise** *people about diet and exercise; her* **advice** *is always excellent and sound.*

Affect, effect: *Affect* is a verb meaning *to influence* or *change.*
Effect is a noun meaning *result* or *consequence.*
The European conquest of the Americas **affected** *world history profoundly. The* **effect** *on the indigenous population was devastating.*

Among, between: Traditionally, *between* has been used with two and *among* has been used with more than two. **Note:** The root *-tween* comes from the word *twain,* meaning *two.*
Between *you and me, who* **among** *our people wants to live on Mars?*

Amount, number: Use *amount* for substances that cannot be counted. Use *number* for items that can be counted.
Bill Gates has an obscene **amount** *of money. He has quite a* **number** *of employees working for him.*

Assure, insure, ensure: *as-* means to promise or say with confidence:
I **assure** *you that I am quite serious about quitting.*

in- means to issue a policy:
We must **insure** *the new house against all natural disasters.*

en- means to make certain something will/won't happen:
Your cruelty will **ensure** *your demise.*

Avenge, revenge: They can be used interchangeably as verbs. As a verb, *avenge* is more common, and *revenge* is often used as a noun. As a verb, *avenge* means to inflict punishment as an act of retribution. *Revenge* as a noun means inflicted pain or retaliation for real or perceived wrongdoings.

*Pauline **avenged** her father's murder by finding the culprit and bringing him to justice.*

*Pauline is seeking **revenge** for her father's murder.*

Bare, bear: *Bare* is an adjective that means uncovered, naked or exposed.

*Don't go out with your neck **bare**. You will catch a cold.*

***Bare** pipes will freeze if left exposed in the winter.*

Bear means to carry, to endure or tolerate, or to maintain a direction. The word *bear* also refers to the animal.

*The Millers came **bearing** expensive gifts.*

*The field **bears** vegetation every season.*

*Who will **bear** the responsibility of raising the children?*

***Bear** left onto Highway 285.*

*We saw a large brown **bear** in the woods.*

Bored, board: *Bored* is the past tense of the verb bore, which means to dig or to cause boredom. *Board* is a small piece of lumber, a flat piece of material. As a verb, it means to cover with boards or to enter.

*The opera left him **bored** to tears.*

*The hammer split the **board** into three separate pieces.*

*To **board** the bus, you need a Metro Card.*

Choose, chose, choice: The past tense of the verb *choose* is *chose*. The noun is *choice.*

*We **choose** what we want.*

*We **chose** what we wanted yesterday.*

*That was our **choice**.*

Conscience, conscious: *Conscience* is the internal ethical voice. *Consciousness* is awareness.

*Although she was **conscious** of what she had done, her **conscience** never bothered her.*

Correct, right: The distinction between the two words is subtle, in that *correct* implies that the given answer(s) is definitive or absolute, like with math and science problems. Contrastingly, *right* would be better as an answer that may simply be considered a matter of opinion, even if most people agree.

*Your answer to the problem was **correct**.*

*Am I on the **right** path?* (Using *correct* here would not work.)

Either, neither: both are used to agree with a negative statement.

*I don't like the snow. Me **neither**.*

*I never eat pork. I don't **either**.*

They are also the negative versions of "both" (representing two people or things).

***Neither** of my parents is home tonight.*

*I don't think **either** hat is for sale.*

Note: When deciding which to use, look for the negative word in the sentence (usually "not"). If there is a negative word, use *either*. If not, use *neither*.

*I never liked this book **either**.*

*I don't think **either** professor is coming to the meeting.*

*You don't want to go to the conference? Me **neither**.*

***Neither** of my cousins is coming to my graduation.*

Farther, further: *Far-* refers only to distance in space. *Fur-* refers to an extent in either time or space.

*There will be no **further** discussion about traveling any **farther** today.*

Fewer, many, less, much: Use *fewer* and *many* for items that can be counted. Use *less* and *much* for substances that cannot be counted.

*The **fewer** hours you work, the **less** money you will make.*

***Many** people are asked to do **much less** work.*

E.g., i.e.: The Latin abbreviation *e.g.* stands for "for example." The abbreviation *i.e.*, stands for "that is."

*He has lots of famous manuscripts, **e.g.**, "Autumn" by John Keats.*

Note: In formal writing, replace *e.g.* with "for example."

*For the exam tomorrow, just bring the necessities, **i.e.**, a pen and paper.*

Etc. The abbreviation of *et cetera* (Latin for "and so forth."). Do not write "and etc."

*She is always looking for love in the wrong places: bars, hotel lobbies, the Internet, **etc.***

Note: *etc.* is frequently abused. Use sparingly.

Good, well: *Good* is an adjective and *well* is an adverb.

*If you perform **good** deeds, life will treat you **well**.*

Grab, grasp, grip: For *grab* there is movement involved and it is fast and fairly desperate. It means to reach out your hand and to *grip* or *grasp* something.

*I tried to **grab** my friend's arm, but he still fell off the balcony.*

Grasp also implies movement, but it is not necessarily desperate.

*My son reached up and **grasped** my arm.*

Grip means to have a strong hold on something.

*His **grip** feels like a vice.*

*My mother has a very firm **grip**.*

Have, of: When we speak, the contraction for the helping verb *have* sounds like the preposition *of*, so some people mistakenly write *of* when they really mean *'ve*.

Incorrect: ***could of** danced, **might of** eaten*

Correct: ***could've** danced, **might've** eaten*

We recommend writing out the complete verb: *could have* danced, *might have* eaten.

Hung, hanged: *hung* is the past tense of hang in most of the verb's tenses.
*Yesterday, she **hung** the plant from the ceiling. Paul hung his head in shame.*

The exception comes when hang means to put someone to death by hanging. The participle in this sense is *hanged*.

*The criminal was **hanged** to death.*

Ideal, idea: "Ideal" refers to absolute perfection or an honorable principle or aim. "Idea" is a thought, a personal view, or an intention.

*To many, Kendrick Lamar is the **ideal** Hip Hop artist.*

*The **ideas** Lamar expresses in his lyrics are profound.*

*You are an **ideal** student because your **ideas** are brilliant.*

It's, its: *It's* is a contraction for "it is." *Its* is a possessive, showing ownership.
*I know **it's** highly unlikely, but I believe she is **its** owner.*

Knew, new: *K-* means to be acquainted with, to know, identify, be subject to.
*I **knew** the answer was wrong.*
*Anon **knew** it was the wrong answer.*
New means for the first time, in original condition, strange.
*Karen bought a **new** purse last week.*
*Tomorrow is a **new** day.*

Know, no: The verb *know* means to be aware, to be informed, to recognize or understand; to be acquainted with.
*Simone did not **know** any of the other mothers at the meeting.*
*If you don't **know** the answer, raise your hand.*

No functions as an adjective, adverb, or an interjection, and it can also be used to give force to a negative statement.
***No**, I will not be quiet.*
*For the last time, the answer is **no**!*
*There is **no** person on earth who has tasted every ethnic cuisine.*

Lay, lie: *Lay* means to put something down (past tense is *laid*). *Lie* means to recline (past tense is *lay*) or to tell a fib (past tense is *lied*).
*I **lay** down my blanket. I **laid** down my blanket. I am **laying** down my blanket.*
*I **lie** in the grass. I **lay** in the grass. I am **lying** in the grass.*
*I often **lie** to spare people's feelings. Yesterday, I **lied** to my boss. I am **lying** to you right now.*

Lead, lead, led: *Lead* (rhymes with bed) is a metal; *lead* (rhymes with reed) means to provide direction or guidance; and *led* is the past tense of *lead*.
*He hit me with a **lead** pipe.*
*My teacher once told me that I should **lead, follow, or get out of the way**.*
*He **led** me to greatness.*

Loose, lose: *Loose* is an adjective meaning not tight, unfastened, or free.
*My daughter's tooth is **loose**.*

Lose is a verb meaning to misplace or to no longer have. It also means the opposite of to win.
*Don't **lose** your sense of humor.*

Pare, pair, pear: *Pare* is to trim, cut away, remove portions of; a *pair* is two similar or corresponding things that are used together; *pear* is an edible fruit.

*After you peel a **pear**, you should **pare** it for dessert.*

***Pare** down the budget.*

***Pare** your Christmas list to a reasonable amount of gifts, like a comfortable **pair** of new sneakers.*

Past, passed: *Past* locates something in time and, often, in space. It can be used as an adjective, noun, or adverb.

*The time for mourning our loss has now **past**.*

*In the **past**, life was more complicated.*

*The dog ran **past** the house.*

Passed is the past participle of the verb "to pass." To pass means to proceed, move forward, depart.

*The vacation **passed** quickly.*

*I **passed** the test.*

*She **passed** the ball and scored the winning goal.*

Peak, peek, pique: *Peak* is a topmost point, or to reach that point. *Peek* is a glance or quick look. *Pique* means to upset or excite someone.

*Currently, the company is at **peak** demand.*

*The movie theater offered a sneak **peek** of Denzel Washington's new film.*

*The book didn't quite **pique** my interest.*

Perspective, prospective: *Per-* is almost always a noun. It refers to the view or angle from which something is viewed; the appearance of objects in relation to each other. *Pro-* is an adjective that means likely to happen or become.

*From the manager's **perspective**, the promotion process was fair.*

*The next chapter provides a historical **perspective** on the early years of the nation's development.*

*She is a **prospective** Yale University student.*

Note: *Prospective* is NOT a word.

Pleaded, pled: *–aded* is the standard past tense of the past participle of the verb *plea*. Both spellings of the word mean to argue a case or cause (frequently used in a court of law), and to make a plea or argue for or against a claim. *–ed* is frequently considered incorrect, but it is so commonly used in American, British, and Canadian languages that it is now considered an accepted alternative form. To be safe, use the always acceptable *–aded* spelling.

*The convicted felon **pleaded** his case to the jury."*

Precede, proceed: *Pre-* means to go in front of or before. *Pro-* means to go forward, to continue.

*Thoughts should always **precede** words.*

*His stroke was **preceded** by a mild heart attack.*

*Burt will **proceed** to the next round of the spelling bee.*

Note: preceed is NOT a word.

Prescribe, Proscribe: *Pre-* means to set down as a rule or to order the use of. *Pro-* is almost the complete opposite, meaning to ban, forbid, or denounce.

*The doctor **prescribed** Zantac for my acid reflux.*

*The government decided to **proscribe** the import of beef.*

Principal, principle: *-pal* means primary or chief and is either used as a noun or an adjective. *-ple* is always used as a noun and generally refers to a rule of law or general truth.

*Mrs. James is the **principal** of my high school.*

*The **principal** goal is to win the election.*

*The leader honored his **principles**.*

Quiet, quite, quit: *-iet* (noun) means noiseless or peaceful. *-iet* (verb) means to make or become quiet. *-ite* (an adverb) means rather or somewhat. *-it* (verb) means to stop or cease.

*If you can **quiet** the twins so that they **quit** crying and **quiet** down, I will **quite** welcome the resulting **quiet**.*

Rise, raise: *Rise* is an irregular verb and intransitive, meaning to move upward without assistance, to return. *Raise* is a regular verb and is transitive, meaning to lift, elevate, or increase.

*In horror movies, zombies **rise** from the dead.*

*Heru **raised** his hand to get the teacher's attention.*

Sense, since: *Sense* is a verb meaning feel or a noun meaning intelligence. *Since* is often associated with time, particularly something that happened in the past. It is commonly used as an adverb to express something that occurred previously but whose effects continue to the present.

*The cat's nose can **sense** danger.*

Since he nearly died on the boat, Brandon has had a fear of the ocean.

*She has been like this **since** high school.* **Note:** Here, it is used in a preposition in referring to an event that has been constant since a past event or time frame.

*Since the revolution, the writers developed their creative **sense**.*

Sore, soar: *-re* refers to aches, pains, and anger. *-ar* is more uncommon and means to swoop or glide through the air, or move upward.

*Althea works all day, so her feet are very **sore**.*

*The temperature will **soar** into the 90s tomorrow.*

*Because he **soared** off the roof and hit the ground, his hip is going to be **sore**.*

Than, then: *Than* is the comparative word.

*The book is better **than** the movie.*

Then is an adverb indicating a point in time.

*And **then** what happened? What did you do **then**?*

That, which: Use the pronoun *that* for restrictive (i.e., essential) clauses and *which* for nonrestrictive (i.e., nonessential) clauses. **See page 25.**

*The dog **that** has rabies ran through my backyard, **which** is not fenced in.* **Note:** *Which* should only begin a sentence if it is a question.

Their, there, they're: *Their* shows possession. *There* indicates place or placement. *They're* is a contraction for "they are."

*Be nice to **their** dogs.*

***There** is no place like home.*

***They're** a bunch of bullies.*

Titled, entitled: *Titled* means that something has received such a title, usually from an author.

*The essay **titled** "Men and the Rights of Freedom" is an iconic interpretation of Boyd's book.*

en- means that a person has rights to something.

*Because of her mother's will, the woman was **entitled** to the family house.*

Note: Over time, *entitled*, when it comes to meaning *named*, has become an accepted variant, but *titled* is still the preferred spelling.

To, too: *To* is the preposition, meaning *toward*.

***To** the Lighthouse.*

To also introduces the infinitive.

***To** be or not **to** be.*

Too is an intensifying adverb.

*This test is **too** difficult.*

Too is also an adverb meaning *also*.

*I **too** have watched the sun come up in the morning.*

Unsatisfied, dissatisfied: *Un-* refers to the feeling of needing more. *Dis-* expresses or shows a lack of satisfaction; to be not pleased or satisfied.

*After eating the meal, he still felt **unsatisfied**.*

*Tony was **dissatisfied** with the hotel's cleaning service.*

Weather, whether (or not): *Weather* refers to the climate, as in "Stormy weather." *Whether* (subordinate conjunction) expresses doubt, sometimes by means of an indirect question.

*He asked me **whether** the **weather** would change by the afternoon.*

Weight, wait, await: As a noun, *weight* is a measure of heaviness; as a verb, it means to load down or make heavier. *Wait* means to remain, linger. *Await* means to wait on or expect.

*I am still **awaiting** a call from my doctor, and the **waiting** has made me overeat so much that I have definitely gained **weight**.*

Who, whom: These are relative pronouns. Use *who* for the subjective case and *whom* for the objective case.

***Who** is at the door?*

*To **whom** am I speaking?*

Note: He equals *who* (**He** is at the door); him equals *whom* (I am speaking to **him**).

Whose, who's: *Whose* shows possession. *Who's* is a contraction of "who is."

***Whose** books are these?*

***Who's** afraid of the Big Bad Wolf?*

Worst, worse: Use *worst* if comparing multiple things: *The first two remakes were bad, but this latest one is the **worst**.*

Use *worse* if you are comparing two things: *I think the remake was **worse** than the original, but that is just my opinion.*

Keep in mind that *worst* refers to the most extreme degree, while *worse* refers to inferior quality or poorer condition.

Your, you're: *-r* shows possession. *-'re* is a contraction for "you are."

***You're** the reason **your** cat is fat.*

words?

Just as words and the meaning of words have changed over time, so too has the use of words, letters, and symbols. Technology and our evolving global society have created a new way of communicating. This is excellent because it brings us all closer together, but it's problematic in that the constant change makes it difficult to remember what to say and how to say it. As such, you must learn to distinguish between what is appropriate for academic writing and informal speak.

Acronyms and Abbreviations: The following list contains acronyms (letters that stand for words) and abbreviations (shortened versions of words):

IMO (In my opinion), **EOD** (End of discussion), **BRB** (Be right back), **BTW** (By the way), **FAQ** (Frequently asked questions), **GF** (Girlfriend), **ROTFLO** (Rolling on the floor laughing out loud), **TMI** (Too much information), **LOL** (Laughing out loud), **OMG** (Oh my God), **IDK** (I don't know)

Note: While commonly used in texting and casual speak, these are not words. They are abbreviations for words and, thereby, are not acceptable in standard essay writing.

FYI (For your information), **ASAP** (As soon as possible), **RSVP** (Translated from the French language, it means "please respond"), **POTUS** (President of the United Sates), **FLOTUS** (First Lady of The United States), **U.S.A.** (United States of America), **U.S.** (United States), **CIA** (Central Intelligence Agency), FBI (Federal Bureau of Investigations), **INTERPOL** (International Criminal Police Organization), **Ex** (Example), **UN** (United Nations), **Rep** (Representative), **Temp** (temporary), **Max** (Maximum), **Min** (Minimum), **AC** (Air Conditioner)

Note: These acronyms and abbreviations have become commonly acceptable in formal writing. Here, the decision to use them is a matter of knowing your audience.

Letters: Sometimes, a letter or series of letters are used as substitutes for a word. These are informal and should NEVER be used in academic writing.

C = see, **R** = are, **B** = be, **G** = gee, **K** = ok, **U** = you, **Y** = why?, **xoxo** = love, **IC** = I see, **PPL** = people, **PRT** = party, **QT** = cutie, **THX** = thanks

Numbers: At times, numbers are used as word substitutes. Again, these should not be used in formal writing.

2 = too, two, **Gr8** = great, **b4** = before, **h8u** = hate you, **4** = for, **L8r** = later, **U2** = you too, **W8** = wait, **No1** = No one

Symbols: @ = at, # = number

1 2 3 4 5

Grammar and Syntax

rules of engagement for writing

Now that you understand the importance of choosing the correct words to convey meaning, it is important for you to learn how to string or group words together effectively. To accomplish this, you must learn the rules of grammar (the logical relationship of words) and syntax (how best to connect sentence elements).

When we say that the grammar is correct, we mean that the relationship among words makes logical sense. When we say that the grammar is faulty, we mean that there is a break in logic.

Example: *They is going to see Justin Timberlake and Jay Z in concert.*

Here you have an agreement problem. The doer (performer of the action) is plural, but the action is singular.

The sentence should read: *They are going to see Justin Timberlake and Jay Z in concert.*

Since grammar is the study of how words interact, the responsibility of the writer is to choose the correct words every time; moreover, the writer must ensure that each word relates to the surrounding words logically (syntax).

parts of speech

NOUN

A word that names a person, place, thing, or idea.

Proper noun: names a specific individual; it is, therefore capitalized.

Dr. James, a turtle named Diggle, The City University of New York, Tillary Street, Africa, Europe, December

Common noun: a non-specific person, place, or thing; it is, therefore, not capitalized.

the nurse, a cat, the school, the car, the book, the day

Appositive: a noun phrase that renames a noun or pronoun.

*Diggle, **my pet turtle**, enjoys being petted.* (See Appositive Phrase on page 25)

PRONOUN

A noun substitute. It can, therefore, do anything that a noun can do.

The moment David met Anne, he really liked her.

He replaces the noun David, and her replaces the noun Anne.

Antecedent: the noun that a pronoun replaces.

The moment David met Anne, he really liked her.

David is the antecedent of the pronoun he. Anne is the antecedent of the pronoun her.

Types of Pronouns

CASE	SUBJECT	OBJECT	POSSESSIVE	POSSESSIVE
1. Personal pronouns				
Singular				
First person	I	me	my	mine
Second person	you	you	your	yours
Third person				
masculine	he	him	his	his
feminine	she	her	her	hers
neuter	it	it	its	its
Plural				
First person	we	us	our	ours
Second person	you	you	your	yours
Third person	they	them	their	theirs

2. Interrogative pronouns — A pronoun that starts a question.

__Which__ woman wants to dance?

Singular and Plural				
who	whom	whose	whose
which	which		
what	what		
whoever	whomever		
whichever	whichever		
whatever	whatever		

3. Relative pronouns — A pronoun that links one phrase or clause to another.

I will support you, __whichever__ decision you make.

Same as interrogative pronouns, plus

that	that

Take a job __that__ you really like.
(**that** acts as subject of the dependent clause)

Take a book __that__ you will enjoy.
(**that** acts as direct object of the dependent clause)

Note: Also see section on conjunctions.

4. Reflexive pronouns — A pronoun that refers to the subject of the sentence.

The dog licks __himself__ every chance he gets.

Singular	***Plural***
myself	ourselves
yourself	yourselves
himself	themselves
herself	
itself	
oneself	

Note: Avoid "theirself" or "theirselves" as these are not words.

5. Demonstrative pronouns — A pronoun that identifies or points to a noun.

__This__ is unacceptable. __These__ shoes are my favorite.

this	these
that	those

Vague or Confusing Pronouns

A single vague pronoun can render an entire sentence meaningless. Therefore, check your writing for any of the following sources of confusion.

No antecedent noun in the sentence or in the immediately preceding ones.

Sometimes, I grow weary of their behavior.

Who is the "I" in the sentence growing weary of? Co-workers? Friends? Pets? The sentence must use a specific noun in order to convey meaning.

Sometimes, I grow weary of my sisters' behavior.

Disagreement (inconsistency) of number:

Disagreement between a pronoun and its antecedent—

An employee would never quit their jobs if their needs were being met.

The employee is singular; the pronoun *their* is plural. **To make them consistent, either turn the noun into a plural word:**

Employees would never quit their jobs if their needs were met.

Or write a singular pronoun:

My employee will never quit her job as long as her salary needs are met.

Exercises

Sharpening Vague or Confusing Pronouns

First, find the trouble spot and then rewrite the sentence, correcting the error. You will find that there is often more than one way to do so.

1. On quiz shows, they often give away valuable prizes.

2. In the bursar's office, they told me to fill out three forms.

3. Parents of sickly children should consider changing their eating habits.

4. My supervisor gives you a really hard time.

5. People waiting for the arrival of an airplane may find it tiresome.

VERB

Indicates either an action or a state of being.

Action Verb

*Shoshana **fell** off of the wagon.*

State-of-Being Verb

*I **am** hungry.*

Helping Verb

A word such as *be, can, have, do,* or *will* that combines with a verb to modify its meaning.

*I **am** becoming angry.*

*He **can** run the store by himself.*

FYI

> The forms of *have, do,* and *be* change form to indicate tense:
>
> have, has, had
>
> do, does, did
>
> be, am, is, are, was, were, being, been
>
> The following helping verbs known as **modals** do not change form to indicate tense:
>
> can, could, may, might, must, shall, should, will, would, ought to

Tense

Every action or state of being occurs at, or within, a period of time. **Verb tense** means the time when an action or state of being occurs. In English, there are six verb tenses. Here is a useful chart.

Verb Tenses

Active Voice, Indicative Mood

Subject is the doer of the action, or the be-er of the state of being.

TENSE	TONE—SIMPLE *Examples*	TONE—CONTINUING OR PROGRESSIVE *Examples*
Present	1. I drive (walk) to work. S/he drives (walks) to work.	I am driving to work. S/he is walking to work.
Present perfect	I have driven to work for six months. S/he has walked to work each day for six months.	I have been driving to work for weeks. S/he has been walking.
Past	I drove to work. S/he walked to work.	I was driving to work. S/he was walking.
Past perfect	I had driven (had walked) for twenty minutes before I discovered that I was on the wrong road.	I had been driving (walking) for twenty minutes before I realized that I was on the wrong road.
Future	1. I will/shall drive (walk) to work. 2. I drive (walk) to work tomorrow.	1. I will/shall be driving (walking). . . 2. I am driving (walking) to work tomorrow.
Future perfect	I will/shall have driven (walked) many miles before I arrive tomorrow.	I will/shall have been driving (walking) for six hours before I arrive tomorrow.

Passive Voice, Indicative Mood: The Usable Forms

Subject is the receiver of the action.

TENSE	TONE—SIMPLE *Examples*	TONE—CONTINUING OR PROGRESSIVE *Examples*
Present	Angelica is (gets) driven to school every day.	Angelica is being (getting) driven to school.
Present perfect	Angelica has been driven to school.	Angelica has been getting driven to school. (rarely used)
Past	Angelica was (got) driven to school.	Angelica was being (getting) driven to school.
Past perfect	Angelica had been driven to school.	Angelica had been getting driven to school. (rarely used)
Future	Angelica will/shall be (get) driven to school.	
Future perfect	Angelica will have been driven to school.	

Note: Since *to walk* in the active voice cannot be followed by a direct object—that is, since *to walk* is an intransitive verb—it has no passive voice.

ADJECTIVE

Modifies or describes a noun or pronoun.

*The **scary** creature terrified the **unsuspecting** teen couple in the film.*

Restrictive and Non-Restrictive Modifiers

A **restrictive modifier** is an adjectival phrase or clause that follows a noun and **is necessary to complete the meaning of the noun**. Because the sentence will not make sense without it, **the restrictive modifier is not set off by commas**.

Prepositional phrase:

*The map **of Africa** requires frequent updating.*

(Without *of Africa*, we would not know which map. We would probably assume that the writer meant the map of the world.)

Adjectival clause:

*The little boy **who fell off his bike** is crying for his mother and father.*

(Without *who fell off his bike*, we would not know which little boy or why he was crying.)

*My neighbor **who lives across the street** is not very social.*

(Without the modifier, we would not know which neighbor. The modifier distinguishes her from all the other neighbors in the neighborhood.)

A **non-restrictive modifier** is an adjectival phrase or clause that follows a noun and merely **gives additional information** about the noun. If the non-restrictive modifier is removed, the sentence will still make sense. Therefore, **a non-restrictive modifier is set off by commas** (see page 53).

Appositive/Gerundive Phrase:

*Autism, **once considered a hopeless condition**, is now being treated in a variety of experimental ways.*

*Throughout history, human beings, **the supposed superior species**, have always dominated animals.* (Removing the appositive will not distort he sentence's meaning)

FYI

To test whether a modifier is restrictive or non-restrictive, read the sentence without the modifier. If the meaning of the sentence is changed or unclear, the modifier is restrictive and you should **not** set it apart with commas. If the meaning of the sentence is unchanged, the modifier is non-restrictive and you **do** need commas.

ADVERB

Modifies a verb, an adjective, an adverb, or a whole clause. Most (but not all) adverbs are formed by adding -ly to an adjective.

Modifying a verb:

*Charlene runs **well**.*

*She will **probably** win a gold medal.*

Modifying an adjective:

*Clara is a strong runner. She will **likely** go to the Olympics someday.*

Modifying another adverb:

*She ice skates **exceptionally** quickly, too.*

Modifying a whole clause:

***Altogether**, she is a remarkable athlete.*

PREPOSITION

Relates one noun or pronoun to another.

*The dog is **on** the porch.*

(In this example, the preposition ***on*** shows the relationship between the dog and the porch.)

The noun that follows the preposition is called the **object of the preposition**.

Together the preposition and its object make up the **prepositional phrase**.

FYI

Words that are commonly used as prepositions:

into	onto	through	unlike
like	out of	throughout	until
near	outside	to	unto
next to	over	toward	up
of	past	under	with
off	since	underneath	within, without
on	than		

Note: Some of these words are also used as adverbs or subordinate conjunctions.

CONJUNCTIONS

Coordinating Conjunction

Connects two or more words, phrases, clauses, or sentences.

I wanted to take piano lessons as a child, **but** *my mother wanted me to take singing lessons instead.*

Note: Comma followed by FANBOY separates the two distinct independent clauses.

I have traveled to China **and** *Japan.*

Note: There is no comma because it is compound.

FYI

Coordinating Conjunctions
"FANBOYS"

For

And

Nor

But

Or

Yet

So

Subordinating Conjunction

Connects a dependent clause with an independent clause; a dependent clause depends on the independent clause and cannot stand alone as a sentence.

(Dependent Clause)   (Independent Clause)
When *Rajesh was ten-years-old, he entered his first chess tournament.*
(For more examples, see pages 31, 40, 41, 43, 52, 53.)

FYI

Words that can be used as subordinating conjunctions:

when, before, after, as, while, since, if, unless, because, although, even though, despite

Exercises

Create three different compound sentences using three different coordinating conjunctions.

Create three different complex sentences using three different subordinating conjunctions.

Create a compound/complex sentence.

Relative Pronoun

A pronoun that, like a subordinate conjunction, joins two clauses in such a way that they are unequal; one clause depends upon the other and cannot stand alone as a sentence.

*I need to find someone **who** can teach me to drive.*

FYI

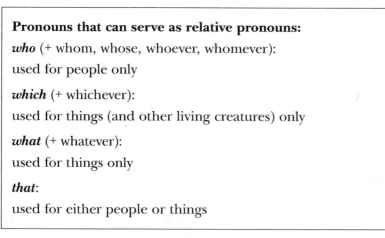

Pronouns that can serve as relative pronouns:

who (+ whom, whose, whoever, whomever):
used for people only

which (+ whichever):
used for things (and other living creatures) only

what (+ whatever):
used for things only

that:
used for either people or things

Who, which, what, and that can be singular or plural.

Who is your best friend?

Who are your colleagues?

*Maurice **is a person who** is always grouchy.*

*The newly elected Senator is one of **the people who are making** a difference.*

*This is one of the beliefs **which have altered** the course of human history.*

*In **what world** is this behavior acceptable?*

*These are the **times that try** men's souls.*

transitions

Conjunctive Adverbs

Words that serve as a transition within or between independent clauses. They can also can be used to establish transition between paragraphs.

Mei wants to go to design school. ***However,*** *her parents would like her to join the family law practice.*

Mei, ***however,*** *is determined to follow her own path.*

The family is planning to pay her a handsome salary if she graduates from law school; ***however,*** *money does not matter to Mei.*

FYI

> **Conjunctive adverbs:**
>
> Accordingly, additionally, also, anyway, besides, certainly, consequently, contrastingly, conversely, finally, furthermore, hence, however, incidentally, indeed, instead, likewise, meanwhile, moreover, nevertheless, next, nonetheless, otherwise, similarly, specifically, still, subsequently, then, therefore, thus

FYI

> **Transitional phrases**
>
> After all, as a matter of fact, as a result, at any rate, at the same time, as such, even so, for example, for instance, in addition, in conclusion, in fact, in other words, in the first place, on the contrary, on the other hand, said differently, so much so

Note: the only difference between conjunctive adverbs and transitional phrases is that conjunctive adverbs are adverbs and, thus, single words. Transitional phrases are actual phrases. However, both are used primarily to establish transition within and between sentences and paragraphs.

I am so confused. So much so, I stopped paying attention ten minutes ago.

Note: when a transitional expression appears between independent clauses, it is preceded by a semicolon and usually followed by a comma.

I am dissatisfied with my working environment; as such, I'll be tendering my resignation at the close of business.

My goal is to live a more fulfilling life; therefore, I am filing for a divorce.

Note: when a transitional expression appears within an independent clause, it usually has commas on either side like an appositive.

While she was uneasy about her role, Farzana performed brilliantly; her sister, subsequently, caught the acting bug, too.

Note: see semicolon on page 54.

INTERJECTION

A word or phrase that is grammatically unrelated to the rest of the sentence but expresses emotion or surprise.

Interjections are punctuated variously:

Damn! *I have a hangover.*

Oh my God! *The house is on fire.*

parts of a sentence

The Parts of a Sentence
Subject   Predicate (verb)   Object   Clause   Phrase   Modifier

SUBJECT (NOUN OR PRONOUN)

With a verb in the active voice, the subject is the doer of the action or the be-er of the state-of-being.

Subject of an action verb:

Mary *threw the ball to John.*

Subject of a state-of-being verb:

We *are very hungry.*

With a verb in the passive voice, the subject is the receiver of the action.

*The **ball** was thrown to John by Mary.*

*Your **complaint** has been filed.*

PREDICATE VERB

The complete verb, which indicates the action or state-of-being of the clause or sentence.

Action verb, active voice:

*Mary **threw** the ball to John.*

*She **has** not **been throwing** the ball for long.*

Action verb, passive voice:

*The poem **was** first **published** in 1600.*

OBJECT (NOUN OR PRONOUN)

Direct Object

With an action verb in the active voice, the direct object is the receiver of the action.

*Mary threw the **ball** to John.*

Indirect Object

The receiver of the direct object.

*Mary threw **John** the ball.*

*Germaine wrote her **mother** a letter.*

CLAUSE

A group of words containing a subject and a predicate verb.

There are two kinds of clauses:

Independent (also called **Main** or **Major**) Clause

Can stand alone as a sentence. Two independent clauses can be connected by a coordinating conjunction (FANBOYS). This is known as coordination (see box on page 27).

Independent clause: *My mother holds two jobs.*

Coordinate clauses: *My mother holds two jobs, **and** I work after school.*

Dependent (also called **Subordinating Clause**)

Cannot stand alone as a sentence. A dependent clause relies on an independent clause to complete its meaning. They are introduced by a subordinating conjunction (see box on page 27).

Introduced by a subordinate conjunction:

***If** I were a rich man, I would quit my job immediately.*

***Since** I am the instructor, you will do as I say.*

*You will do as I say **since** I am the instructor.*

PHRASE

A group of words without a subject and predicate verb.

Prepositional Phrase

Composed of a preposition and its object. It is used as a **modifier** (adjective or adverb).

Adjective (modifying the noun *sound*):
*The sound **of music** is lovely.*

Adverb (modifying the verb *ran*):
*He ran **like lightning**.*

Adverb (modifying the whole clause):
***Without doubt**, Cho is capable.*

Participle, Participial Phrase

A participle is a part of a verb. It is used with a helping verb to form a complete verb.

is writing:	*is*	= helping verb	*writing*	= participle (present)
had written:	*had*	= helping verb	*written*	= participle (past)

On its own, however, a participle is never a verb. We do not, for example, say: *She writing to her cousin.*

When used alone, without a helping verb, a participle (or a participial phrase) can function as either an adjective or a noun.

***Thinking quickly**, I ran for my life.*

*The **thinking** woman has an advantage over her enemy.*

A participle used as a noun is called a **gerund**.

Gerund (present participle only):
***Swimming** relaxes her.*
*(Subject of **relaxes**)*

Gerund phrase:
***Healing the sick** is a worthy profession.*
*(Subject of **is**)*

*He is in the habit of **doing his homework neatly**.*
*(Object of the preposition **of**)*

Infinitive, Infinitive Phrase

The infinitive is the name of a verb, formed by the word *to* plus the verb.

to be, to do

The infinitive, or an infinitive phrase, can function as a noun:

To err *is human.*

(Subject of *is*)

The children want **to finish their homework** *before dinner.*

(Direct object of *want*)

Or as a modifier (adjective or adverb):

To write a polished essay, *one must proofread.*

(Adjective modifying the pronoun *one*)

The question is hard **to formulate.**

(Adverb modifying the adjective *hard*)

Modifiers

A word or phrase that modifies or adds information to other parts of a sentence. Adjectives, adverbs, and many phrases and clauses are modifiers.

Any student **who does not do his or her homework** *will fail.*

types of sentences

There are varied definitions for a simple sentence. For example, "Run!" is actually a single word sentence. However, the basic definition for a sentence is a group of words that has a subject as well as a predicate, and they all come together to express a complete thought. Keep in mind, the predicate may have modifiers.

Jahman loves his new apartment.

Four Sentence Purposes:

Declarative Sentence

Makes a statement; imparts information.

I want to win the Lotto badly.

Interrogative Sentence

Asks a question.

What book are you reading?

Imperative Sentence

Gives a command; makes a demand.

Open the window and shut the door.

Note: Often in an imperative sentence, the subject of the verb is understood to be *you* even though it is not stated.

Exclamatory Sentence

Exclaims (with or without an exclamation mark.)

What utter nonsense!

I can't believe it.

sentence structures

Simple Sentence

Has one independent clause only.

Alex has already made an outline for the paper due on Tuesday.

Compound Sentence

Has two or more independent clauses (each joined to the one before it by a coordinate conjunction or a semicolon).

She is writing the rough draft today, but she will wait until tomorrow to proofread it. (see page 27)

He wanted justice; he dispensed vengeance. (see page 54)

Complex Sentence

Has one independent clause and one or more dependent clauses.

After she has edited the first draft of her paper, she will type the final draft.

Compound-Complex Sentence

Has two or more independent clauses and one or more dependent clause(s).

When she comes home from work, Sara will proofread the final draft of her paper for oversights, but she will probably not find many.

parsing sentences

Each word in a sentence is logically connected to all the other words in the sentence, and usually in more than one way. Let us look at all the logical relationships among the words in the following sentence.

Kubie begrudgingly gave her opinion at the office meeting despite the fact that no one takes her seriously.

FYI

Parts of Speech

Proper Noun: Kubie

Adverbs: begrudgingly, seriously

Verbs: gave, takes

Possessive Pronoun: her

Common nouns: opinion, meeting, fact

Preposition: at

Article: the

Adjective: office

Subordinating Conjunction: despite

Pronoun: no one

FYI

Parts of Sentence

Subject (of Independent Clause): Kubie

Verb (of Independent Clause): gave

Direct Object: her opinion

Modifier: begrudgingly

Prepositional phrase: at the office meeting

Dependent clause: despite the fact that no one takes her seriously

Subject (of Dependent Clause): no one

Verb (of Dependent Clause): takes

Exercises

Identifying Subjects, Predicate Verbs, and Sentence Types

In the following excerpt from Julian Williams' "The New Breed," identify independent and dependent clauses (write IC or DC above the sentence). Next, circle the subject and underline the verb for each clause. Lastly, identify the sentence type.

I was in the midst of telling the cops how she and her friends were waiting for me and how I was just defending myself when I began to sweat uncontrollably. The more and more I said, the more my nerves frayed.

And then I lost it.

I rambled off about how she had held the train hostage. Now moving my hands excitedly, I told them about how much of an adult I am and how she was just a dirty train spitter. I told them how nobody cared about her and how she was just lashing out and that this wasn't my fault. I mean, her fault. I tried to tell them how she was unloved and poor and under-educated and how no one cared and how she shared a room with several siblings and how no one had ever spun her on the balls of their feet and how she shouldn't wear white after Labor Day and how the White kids on the train had abandoned her and. . . .

I tried to explain to the police—but I was nervous and angry, so the last forty minutes came out in a flood of emotion. For some reason, I couldn't quite clarify how I'd gotten to the point of hitting her while, at the same time, justify the life she had led that caused her to behave like a savage. Which is why I hit her in the first place. I think. As the ambulance pulled onto the sidewalk to take her away, the police handcuffed me and placed me in the back of the patrol car. I wanted to ask them if they would be so kind as to go and tell my class I wasn't going to make it, but I figured I should probably be quiet for a little while.

sentence errors and how to correct them

The term **faulty syntax** means unconnected or loosely or imprecisely connected sentence elements. Therefore, whatever the particular syntax error is, the solution will lie either in the connections—more connections, tighter ones, or more precise ones—or in the separations.

If you can recognize clauses and conjunctions, and can distinguish them from other sentence elements, then you can proofread your own writing for possible syntax errors.

Here's how:

Focus on one sentence at a time. First, locate every predicate verb and its subject; each set is a clause. If you look at a sentence and can't find even one clause, or if you find only a dependent clause without an independent clause, you probably have a **sentence fragment**.

When more than two clauses appear in a sentence, ask what conjunction (if any) connects each clause to the one before it. Look specifically for a coordinate conjunction, a subordinate conjunction, or a relative pronoun. If you can't find a conjunction joining two clauses (or a semicolon separating them), you probably have a **run-on sentence**.

For fragments and run-ons, sentence length is not the issue. It is possible to write a very long sentence fragment:

On a beautiful day in spring, when the sun was shining and the birds were singing in all the trees, over the river and through the woods to grandmother's house.

or a very short run-on sentence:

You speak she will answer.

At times, even sentences that are grammatically "correct" may fail to communicate your meaning fully. If you find two or more short **choppy sentences** in a row, you have probably not shown all the connections between your ideas. If you find a long **rambling sentence**, in which several clauses are joined by one coordinate conjunction after another, you probably need to show the relationships among the ideas more precisely, either by subordinating one idea to another or by putting different ideas into different sentences. Run-ons, fragments, choppy sentences, and rambling ones look like four different errors, but they are all symptoms of just one problem: **insufficient connections**.

Another family of syntax errors occurs when the ideas in a sentence are connected but the connection is illogical. The result may be **faulty parallelism**, a **dangling modifier**, or a **lost subject**. Whatever the specific error, the solution is some form of **reconnection**.

When you find a syntax error, there is never only one right way to correct it. Furthermore, you can pick and choose not only between absent or illogical connections and precise ones, but also between good connections and even better ones.

SENTENCE FRAGMENT

A "sentence" without an independent clause; that is, a phrase or a dependent clause punctuated as a complete sentence.

Fragment (phrase):

A lovely view of the meadow.

Fragment (dependent clause):

Before she bought a personal computer.

Fragment (dependent clause):

Whenever you need help or advice.

The four ways to correct a sentence fragment are:

1. **Attach** the fragment to the sentence before or after it.

Incorrect: *Tanya sold her electric typewriter. Before she bought a personal computer.*

Correct: *Tanya sold her electric typewriter before she bought a personal computer.*

or

Before she bought a personal computer, Tanya sold her electric typewriter.

2. **Expand** a phrase into a full independent clause.

From his kitchen window, *David has a lovely view of the meadow.*

3. **Add** an independent clause to a free-floating dependent clause.

Incorrect: *Sophie is a true friend. Whenever you need help or advice.*

Correct: *Sophie is a true friend. Whenever you need help or advice, she will be there for you.*

4. **Convert** a dependent clause into an independent clause by dropping the subordinate conjunction or relative pronoun.

Fragment (dependent clause):

Before she bought a personal computer.

Complete sentence (independent clause):

She bought a personal computer.

Exercises

Recognizing and Correcting Fragments

Examine each of the sentences below separately. If it is a complete sentence, label it *S*. If it is only a fragment, label it *F*. In either case, explain why. Then rewrite the whole paragraph in complete sentences.

> We ran. Over the bridge into Brooklyn. Our friends were waiting for us. They knew the story. But wanted us to tell it anyway. It was my fault. Because I asked the wrong girl to dance at the house party. I didn't see her ex-boyfriend or his six friends hiding in the shadows. They gave chase. We took off running past the subway and onto the Brooklyn Bridge. We were fast enough to run. The distance and thankfully they were too slow to catch us.

RUN-ON SENTENCE

A "sentence" containing two independent clauses that are not connected by a coordinate conjunction or separated by a semicolon.

Types of Run-On Sentences

Simple Run-On

The **simple run-on** (also called **fused**) **sentence**:

I had a boyfriend he left me.

Comma Splice

The **comma splice** (cs), a run-on sentence with only a comma between the two independent clauses:

I had a boyfriend, he left me.

A comma cannot separate two independent clauses; only a period or semicolon can do that. Think of the period or semicolon as a red light, signaling a full stop. Think of the comma as merely a yellow light, or a turn signal.

Note: The comma splice is frequently used in fiction as a creative tool to enhance a character's voice.

Run-On Sentence or Comma Splice with a Conjunctive Adverb

The **run-on sentence** or **comma splice** with a **conjunctive adverb**:

*The authorities disagreed with one another, **therefore** I had to make up my own mind.* (see page 55)

Unlike a true conjunction (a coordinate conjunction, a subordinate conjunction, or a relative pronoun), **a conjunctive adverb cannot connect two clauses inside a sentence. A conjunctive adverb can show a connection only between two separate sentences.**

Fortunately, it is easy to distinguish between a conjunctive adverb and a true conjunction: **a conjunctive adverb can move within its own clause; a true conjunction can't.**

Conjunctive adverb:

*The authorities disagreed with one another; **therefore**, I had to make up my own mind.*

Coordinate conjunction:

*The authorities disagreed with one another, **so** I had to make up my own mind.*

In the sentence above, try moving **so** to any other position in the clause it introduces. What happens?

Subordinate conjunction:

***Since** the authorities disagreed with one another, I had to make up my own mind.*

You can move a whole dependent clause, but you cannot move a subordinate conjunction, by itself, to any other position in its clause. In the sentence above, try moving *Since*, by itself, to any other position in the clause it introduces. What happens?

Run-On Sentence or Comma Splice with an Ordinary Adverb

The **run-on sentence** or **comma splice** with an **ordinary adverb**:

Foster stayed for awhile, then he went home.

If you're not sure whether a word is an ordinary adverb or a conjunction, you can apply the same test as for conjunctive adverbs: **an ordinary adverb can move within its clause; a conjunction can't.**

. . . he then went home.

The three ways to correct a run-on sentence or comma splice: connect (with words), **reduce** (a clause to a phrase), or **separate** (with punctuation).

1. **Connect** the two clauses **with a true conjunction**.

Incorrect (comma splice):

Elissa should have planted wheat, instead she planted cotton.

Coordinate conjunction:

*Elissa should have planted wheat, **but** instead she planted cotton.*

Subordinate conjunction:

***Although** Elissa should have planted wheat, she planted cotton instead.*

Relative pronoun:

*Elissa, **who** should have planted wheat, chose to plant cotton instead.*

Often, one's first impulse is to connect two clauses with the coordinate conjunction *and*. It's a step in the right direction, but don't stop there. Before you settle for *and*, the most general and overworked of conjunctions, take the next step. See whether you can find a tighter connection.

*I had a squirrel, **and** her name was Diggy.*

Relative pronoun:

*I had a squirrel **whose** name was Diggy.*

(Notice that this sentence is not only tighter but, also, one word shorter than the previous one.)

2. **Reduce** one of the clauses to a phrase, or to a part of the independent clause.

One independent clause with a phrase:

*I had a squirrel **named** Diggy.*

*Foster stayed for awhile **before going home**.*

One independent clause, with a single subject and a compound predicate verb:

Foster stayed for awhile and then went home.

Elissa should have planted wheat but instead planted cotton.

3. **Separate** the two clauses **with punctuation**.

If you decide that there really isn't a close connection between the two clauses, then write them as two separate sentences, using a **period**.

The authorities disagreed with one another. Therefore, I had to make up my own mind.

Foster stayed for awhile. Then he went home.

Alternatively, if the two clauses bear an especially close relationship to each other, keep them in the same sentence, but separate them with a **semicolon**.

The authorities disagreed with Elissa; however, she did not replant her crops.

Exercises

Recognizing Run-ons

The following paragraph is made up of independent clauses and run-on sentences. As you read, attempt to distinguish the independent clauses from the run-on sentences. While you are making these distinctions, correct the run-ons as you move from line to line.

Today, I am happy. After a series of rainy days the weather has begun to improve and because of this my spirits have soared. More than this I am also happy about the acceptance letter I received from my number one college choice. I hope to study music and theater and with any luck I'll end up on Broadway with my name up in lights. My parents are very proud of me. The entire family is going to use my Student Orientation weekend as an excuse to take a family vacation where we will gather together as a group. I am very happy about this. I will miss them while I'm away at college even my little brother who usually irritates me. We're a very loving family. My leaving is going to be difficult.

CHOPPY SENTENCES

Too many short sentences in a row.

A string of short sentences probably does not communicate all the connections the writer means to make among the ideas. Furthermore, the overall effect is often dull.

How to recognize choppy sentences:

When you proofread, look for these flashing signals:

Two or more short sentences in a row.

The day was Saturday. The office was closed.

Be especially alert for two short sentences that start or end with the same word, or a pronoun for it.

Karim *needed food.* ***He*** *went to the store.*

Be equally skeptical if the first sentence ends with a word and the second sentence begins with the same word, or a pronoun for it.

Karim went to the grocery ***store****. The* ***store****, however, was closed.*

or

It, however, was closed.

The ways to correct choppy sentences:

1. **Connect** them with a conjunction—a coordinate conjunction, a subordinate conjunction, or a relative pronoun.

Coordinate conjunction:

Karim needed food, ***so*** *he went to the grocery store,* ***but*** *it was closed.*

Subordinate conjunction:

Because *he needed food, Karim went to the store.* (see coordination and subordination on page 27)

Relative pronoun:

Karim, ***who*** *needed food, went to the grocery store.*

2. **Reduce** one of the short sentences to a word or phrase, **and attach** it to the other sentence.

In need of food*, Karim went to the grocery store.*

or

Needing food, . . .

or

To buy food, . . .

3. **Or the sentence can be corrected with a semicolon.**

Karim needed food; he went to the store to buy groceries. (see page 54)

Exercises

Correcting Choppy Sentences

How many different ways can you find to connect the choppy sentences in the brief paragraph below?

> I was angry. They told me I would find true love on the dating service. I didn't make a love connection. The first date was bad. The second date was worse. I got frustrated. I quit trying.

RAMBLING SENTENCE

A long sentence with many independent clauses, all of them connected with coordinate conjunctions.

How to correct a rambling sentence: Establish **coordination**. Or, insert a semicolon and a conjunctive adverb or transitional phrase. (Note: See pages on uses of the semicolon).

Subordinate some of its clauses to others.

When you come to a new thought, start a new sentence.

Exercises

Correct the rambling sentence below.

> To make a refreshing summer drink, first crush about four ice cubes in your blender and then peel a banana and break it into a few pieces and toss them into the blender, and then pour in some fresh or frozen orange juice, and blend all this for about a minute, and then it will be a thick, foamy liquid, and then pour your cold, nourishing drink into a tall glass and enjoy it.

FAULTY CONNECTIONS

Faulty Parallelism

Parallelism means expressing similar ideas in similar grammatical forms.

Look, for example, how this principle applies to the following sentence.

*Charles looks forward **to pursuing** graduate studies, [to] **teaching** French, [to] **running** for office, [to] **raising** children, [to] **cooking** tasty meals, and even [to] **cleaning** house–but not to doing them all at once!*

Logically, comparisons can be made only between similar elements. Elements that are not similar are therefore not comparable.

Incorrect:

An electrician's income is often higher than a teacher.

(An income cannot be compared to a person.)

Correct:

An electrician's income is often higher than a teacher's [income].

or

. . . than that of a teacher.

Note: In the first sentence, *income* is not stated but implied.

Exercises

Correct the following:

1. Amassing power, getting rich, and to attain high status are Alexander's goals in life.

2. The sound of the cello is more resonant than the flute.

3. Fiona enjoys drinking French champagne, dancing till dawn, and she tries to avoid serious emotional attachments.

4. Not only does Joan excel at writing science fiction, but also theater.

5. In addition to a well-structured curriculum, our class went on trips to see the homes of presidents, farm animals, ceramics classes, and museums.

Misplaced (Dangling) Modifier (MM)

The general rule-of-thumb regarding modifiers is that they should appear in your sentence as close as possible to the words that they modify. Otherwise, you may confuse your reader.

Incorrect: *The frog won the race with long legs.*

Does the race have long legs or does the frog?

Correct: *The frog with long legs won the race.*

Correct the following:

Let me know about your party during the holiday.

Small, unobtrusive modifiers are easy to misplace. When you proofread, cast a sharp eye on sneaky little words like *almost, barely, hardly, just, nearly,* and *only*. Consider how the placement of the modifier affects the meaning of the sentence below:

Only the teacher told me that she liked my essay.
(Nobody else told me.)

The *only* teacher told me that she liked my essay.
(There are no other teachers.)

The teacher *only* told me that she liked my essay.
(She did not show me.)

The teacher told *only* me that she liked my essay.
(She told nobody else.)

The teacher told me *only* that she liked my essay.
(That's all she told me.)

The teacher told me that *only* she liked my essay.
(Nobody else liked it.)

The teacher told me that she *only* liked my essay.
(She did not love it.)

The teacher told me that she liked *only* my essay.
(She liked nobody else's.)
                    or
(She liked none of my other work.)

The teacher told me that she liked my *only* essay.
(I've written just one.)

The teacher told me that she liked my essay *only*.
(That was all she liked.)

Dangling Participle

When a sentence begins with a gerundive or a gerundive phrase, the gerundive will modify the first noun or pronoun that follows the comma. If the wrong noun or pronoun follows the comma, the error is called a **dangling participle**.

Incorrect:
Hurrying to school, the ice caused Ian to lose his footing.

(The ice wasn't hurrying.)

Correct:
Hurrying to school, Ian lost his footing on the ice.

A dangling participle can be corrected in two ways:

1. Rearrange the word order, or add some words, so that the noun following the comma is the one you really mean the gerundive to modify. This usually entails changing the independent clause from passive to active voice.

Incorrect: *Barking loudly, the cat was chased by the dog.*
Correct: *Barking loudly, the dog chased the cat.*

Incorrect: *Arriving home, the door was locked.*
Correct: *Arriving home, I found the door locked.*

2. If you can't do that, expand the gerundive phrase into a whole clause.

Incorrect: *Riding my bicycle, the sun set.*
Correct: *As I was riding my bicycle, the sun set.*

Exercises

Correct the following:

1.   Reading that essay, the vague generalizations baffled me.

2.   Listening to Dr. Ramirez, the diagnosis made sense.

3.   After graduating from college, Keisha's grandmother gave her a wrist watch.

4.   Lost in the forest, the night noises frightened us.

5.   Exhilarated by the victory, her feet were walking on air.

1 2 **3** 4 5

Punctuation

If you are going to be an effective communicator, you MUST learn how to use and understand punctuation. The proper use of punctuation is not a small part of writing—it is everything. We write to be read. Essentially, if you omit or misuse punctuation, you are undermining your own creative or scholarly voice; moreover, you may miscommunicate ideas or feelings to your reader or audience. Conversely, if you do not understand how an author is using punctuation, you may miss crucial explication, changes in voice or tone, pivotal and revealing statements and ideas, or misunderstand the author's meaning altogether.

The period (.), comma (,), semicolon (;), colon (:), hyphen (-), and the dash (—), among other forms of punctuation, are not to be feared. They are your friends. Breathe deeply for a moment, and accept that fact. Your job is to learn when and how to use them. The use of punctuation is just like learning how to use the plus and minus signs in mathematics; once you understand their functions and commit them to memory, using them becomes second nature.

Take a moment to peruse the above paragraphs again. You'll find that almost every form of punctuation has been used. If you, the reader, can understand what we've written, then each of the punctuation symbols has been used correctly.

Often in writing, the best way to see the value of punctuation is to remove it. What follows are two versions of a passage from Henry James' *The American*. In the first version, the punctuation has been omitted. The second version is the published excerpt. See if you can correct the first version before reading the second.

Omitted Punctuation:

You have evidently had some surprising adventures you have seen some strange sides of life you have revolved to and fro over a whole continent as I walk up and down the Boulevard You are a man of the world with a vengeance You have spent some deadly dull hours and you have done some extremely disagreeable things you have shoveled sand as a boy for supper and you have eaten roast dog in a gold diggers camp You have stood casting up figures for ten hours at a time and you have sat through Methodist sermons for the sake of looking at a pretty girl in another pew All that is rather stiff as we say But at any rate you have done something and you are something you have used your will and you have made your fortune You have not stupefied yourself with debauchery and you have not mortgaged your fortune to social conveniences You take things easily and you have fewer prejudices even than I who pretend to have none but who in reality have three or four Happy man you are strong and you are free

Published Version:

You have evidently had some surprising adventures; you have seen some strange sides of life, **you have revolved to and fro over a whole continent as I walk up and down the Boulevard**. You are a man of the world with a vengeance! You have spent some deadly dull hours, and you have done some extremely disagreeable things: you have shoveled sand, as a boy, for supper, and you have eaten roast dog in a gold-diggers' camp. You have stood casting up figures for ten hours at a time, and you have sat through Methodist sermons for the sake of looking at a pretty girl in another pew. All that is rather stiff, as we say. But at any rate you have done something *and you are something*; you have used your will *and you have made your fortune*. You have not stupefied yourself with debauchery *and you have not mortgaged your fortune to social conveniences*. You take things easily, and you have fewer prejudices even than I, who pretend to have none, but who in reality have three or four. Happy man, you are strong *and you are free*.

Note on the bolded sentence: Correcting the sentence with the semicolon is not incorrect. In essay writing, this sentence would be considered a comma splice; however, this is a fictive voice and is punctuated as the artist, James, believes his character speaks. (See **comma splice** on page 40.)

Note on italicized sentences: Commas between the coordinating conjunctions would be correct. The reason these sentences do not have commas are, again, because the author felt the fictive voice was better served without the commas, and because the sentences are so succinct, there is no danger of misreading (see **comma** on page 52).

Now try to read the following statement from which all punctuation has been omitted:

The police stopped my brother Taj and his wife Alicia said they were going to the market.

Does this mean:

The police stopped my brother Taj and his wife. Alicia said they were going to the market.

or does it mean:

The police stopped my brother Taj, and his wife, Alicia, said they were going to the market.

or does it mean:

"The police stopped my brother Taj and his wife," Alicia said. "They were going to the market."

Whose brother is Taj anyway? Mine or Alicia's? Only the punctuation can tell.

end punctuation

End punctuation indicates the end of the sentence.

Every sentence ends with a **period** (.), a **question mark** (?), or an **exclamation mark** (!). End punctuation is followed by two spaces.

PERIOD (.)

The **period** is by far the most frequently used end punctuation. It indicates a full stop.

Use it at the end of a declarative sentence (a statement):

New Orleans is a beautiful city.

When an abbreviation falls at the end of a sentence, use only one period.

The Romans invaded Britain in 55 A.D.

QUESTION MARK (?)

The **question mark** is used at the end of a direct question.

Will they serve wine at the party?

In a direct quotation, the question mark ordinarily goes inside the quotation marks.

"How long did it take you to fly here from Miami?" asked Joanne.

Remember that an indirect question is a statement, and therefore ends with a period.

Joanne asked how long it had taken us to fly here from Miami.

A question mark inserted after a fact expresses uncertainty or doubt.

Euripides (480?–406 B.C.) created characters with whom we can sympathize today.

EXCLAMATION MARK (!)

The **exclamation mark** is used after an emphatic statement, command, or interjection.

He can't swim! Save him!

"Aha!" he exulted. "I've caught you at last."

internal punctuation

Internal punctuation marks are followed by one space.

COMMA (,)

The **comma** (,) indicates slight pauses in reading and differentiates sentence parts.

Commas are used in the following situations:

1. Before a coordinating conjunction (FANBOYS) that connects two independent clauses.

Note: The comma always goes before the conjunction, never after it.

The apartment is large, but making it habitable will require a great many repairs.

Anna selected a new iPad, and she didn't even glance at the price tag.

When coordinate clauses are short, the comma can sometimes be omitted.

You go your way and I'll go mine.

2. To separate a dependent clause from the independent clause, especially when the dependent clause comes first.

When Rashid studies, he likes to listen to soft music.

When the independent clause comes first, we often omit the comma between it and the dependent clause.

Rashid likes to listen to soft music when he studies. (Also see page 27)

3. To separate an introductory element—a modifier, or interjection, or conjunctive adverb—from the body of a clause. This is also known as a "lead-in."

Rushing to catch the train, *Dee dropped her briefcase.*

Fortunately, *a kind stranger picked it up and tossed it to her.*

In spite of his aching back, *Ryan planted the new trees.*

As a result, *he had to spend a week in traction.*

Andrew, *please bring me a plate of salad.*

Eventually, *we will succeed.*

4. To separate an insertion (see appositive/gerundive phrase on page 25). An insertion is a word or phrase that can be taken out of a sentence without losing the integrity of the main assertion.

Next weekend, ***no matter what,*** *I'll mow the lawn.*

Dee, ***rushing to catch the train,*** *dropped her briefcase.*

Please, ***Andrew,*** *bring me a plate of salad.*

Don't, ***however,*** *put mayonnaise on it.*

Paul, ***who was hired only last month,*** *has already been made a project manager.*

Note: Recall that insertions of modifying clauses that are **restrictive** (i.e., essential) do not take commas.

Any student who arrives late will be penalized.

5. To separate items in a series.

Sam is warm, sympathetic, and sensitive.

Mary woke up, turned off her alarm clock, rubbed her eyes, and readied her mind for the day ahead.

Note: To decide whether you need commas between adjectives, see whether you can place the word *and* between them.

The hikers walked down a long, steep, stony path.

Nina wore a light blue cashmere sweater.

6. To set off quotations that appear in a sentence.

Irene Keller smiled and said, "Welcome to our forum."

"Thank you for inviting me to speak," replied Dr. Moore.

"After my lecture," Dr. Moore said, "we can have a question-and-answer period."

7. Introductory Clause: Introduces time and or place. The most popular introductory clause of all time is ***Once upon a time,...***

Last year*, I learned how to drive.*

Tomorrow*, I take my final exam.*

8. Generally, anything added to an independent clause can be separated by a comma. (see restrictive and non-restrictive clauses page 25)

The student went to see an academic adviser and, in doing so, rectified the situation.

The student went to see an academic adviser, and, by doing so, the adviser rectified the situation.

SEMICOLON (;)

Uses of the semicolon:

Like a period, a semicolon can be used between two independent clauses, but only if they are especially closely related; then you can think of the semicolon as a silent coordinate conjunction.

Simon does his homework every night; Claudia does hers only when she feels like it.

(Here, the coordinating conjunction might be *but* or *and*.)

Again like a period, a semicolon can be used between two clauses when the second clause begins with a conjunctive adverb.

Simon does his homework every night; however, Claudia does hers only when she feels like it.

When a series is embedded in another series, semicolons divide the items in the larger series, while commas separate the items in the embedded series.

The American colonists wanted three things: the right to life, liberty, and the pursuit of happiness; freedom to trade with other nations besides the mother country; and no taxation without direct representation.

Note: the first independent clause must always be strong and clear; keep in mind, however, that the second independent clause is often dependent upon the first.

Hip Hop is here to stay; it is a genre that every ethnic group can enjoy.

Note: The second independent clause is a complete sentence, but it doesn't make complete sense because the reader needs the subject of Hip Hop to fully understand the point. As such, the second independent clause is dependent on the first.

COLON (:)

Uses of the colon:

To introduce a list.

When elected President, I promise three things: universal health care, troop withdrawal, and lower taxes.

To introduce a definition, an explanation.

We need to ask ourselves one thing: is this really necessary?

To introduce a long or formal quotation, following an independent clause.

Karl Marx is credited with the following words: "Workers of the world, unite! You have nothing to lose but your chains."

Between a title and subtitle:

Looking for the Enemy: the Eternal Internal Gender Wars of our Sisters.

Use between independent clauses if the second summarizes or explains the first. It answers the question *why* or *how*.

Good art is like good wine: it appreciates with age.

DASH (—)

Multifunctional, dashes often highlight, or amplify, the part of the sentence they separate.

The two grumpy old men–they had been neighbors for twenty years–relied on each other more than either of them was willing to admit.

They can also show an abrupt change of thought or tone.

I was wondering when we might–oh my goodness, is that my song playing?

They are also necessary when your appositive phrase has internal commas.

In any country, the basic needs of the people–food, shelter, security, and healthcare–must be met.

PARENTHESES ( )

Use parentheses to enclose words or figures that clarify or are used as an aside.

Tomorrow, I expect to be paid one thousand dollars ($1000).

John asked the speaker (after taking a full minute to compose his thoughts) the question we were all waiting to hear.

The two grumpy old men (they had been neighbors for twenty years) relied on each other more than either of them was willing to admit.

Note: here, the comma or dash would be better form.

Also, parentheses appear throughout writing to indicate in-text citations.

Jones argues, "The true value of democracy rest within the fabric of youthful thinking" (21).

Besides in-text citations, parentheses are often abused and should be used sparingly.

Punctuation after a parenthetical statement goes outside the closing parenthesis.

The committee passed the resolution almost unanimously (with only one dissenting vote).

However, if the entire sentence is in parentheses, then the punctuation goes inside the parentheses. (This sentence is an example.)

THE SLASH (/)

While poetry has its own use of the slash for line breaks, in essay writing it is mainly used to separate paired terms such as pass/fail, producer/director, refresh/reload, Dear Sir/Madam, The American Revolution/Slavery era. With these examples, the marking is often used to indicate "or." The slash is also commonly used to indicate abbreviations: a/c number (account), n/a (not applicable), w/o (without), c/o (care of). And, of course, it is generally used to separate day, month, and year: 12/25/15.

Note: Do not over-use the slash to indicate "or." It looks lazy because the "and/or" construction is widely considered bad form; as such, use sparingly, if at all.

HYPHEN (-)

(Not to be confused with the dash (—))

Uses of the hyphen:

To **join the parts of a compound (hyphenated) word**.

great-grandmother, brother-in-law

self-confidence, self-inflicted

a two-hour class, a two-thirds majority, a four-year-old child

Hyphenate the elements of a compound modifier only if that modifier precedes the noun.

The book is well-written.

This is a well-written book.

Here, these sentences are basically the same, but only the second sentence is correctly hyphenated. When *well-written* comes before *book*, it should be hyphenated. When *well-written* comes after *book*, it should appear as *well written*.

APOSTROPHE (')

Uses of the apostrophe:

To **form contractions**

The apostrophe stands for the letters that are omitted.

I'm the man. (I am the man.)

The Common Contractions			
'm = am	I'm		
're = are	you're	we're	they're
's = is *or* has	he's	she's	it's
	who's	what's	that's
'll = will	I'll	you'll	he'll (etc.)
'd = would	I'd	you'd	she'd (etc.)
've = have	I've	you've	we've (etc.)
n't = not	isn't	aren't	wasn't, weren't
hasn't	haven't	hadn't	
doesn't	don't	didn't	
won't	wouldn't		
can't	couldn't		
shan't	shouldn't		

To **show possession**

Using an apostrophe, we can convert a noun into a possessive adjective or a possessive pronoun.

Lisa's watch keeps excellent time.

Wilbur walked into the boys' locker room.

The view from Mr. Jones' office is spectacular.

Note: Do not use an apostrophe with either plural nouns or possessive pronouns.

Incorrect: *Do you remember that the **teacher's** asked you not to use **you're** cell phone.*

To a word ending in any letter other than *s*, add an apostrophe and an s ('s). This is true whether the word is singular or plural.

car's   house's   everybody's   children's

To any plural word ending in s, just add an apostrophe (').

the houses' lawns   the babies' cribs   the Browns' cabin

When the word ends with s, the apostrophe goes outside the s (s'). When this is done, the 's is implied.

The bus's tires   the bus' tires   Ms. Jones's desk   Ms. Jones' desk

A compound possessive (two or more owners joined by *and*) uses an apostrophe only after the second owner.

Janice drives her father and mother's car. (Both parents own the car.)

Ben and Jerry's ice cream.

Because a reader's understanding may be completely different than the writer's intention, be careful with the possessive apostrophe.

Please go to the house and get Kwasi and Micaela's mail.

Here, the reader should only get the mail that is addressed to both Kwasi and Micaela.

Please go to the house and get Kwasi's and Micaela's mail.

Here, the reader should get all of the mail addressed to Kwasi and all of the mail addressed to Micaela.

capitalization

Capitalize the first word of every sentence and names of people, places, days of the week, and months.

Specific persons (and their titles):

Pablo Picasso, Ida B. Wells, Queen Victoria, President Barack Obama, Doctor Salk, Professor Saddik, Huckleberry Finn

Specific places:

North America, the Pacific Ocean, Lake Huron, Mount Everest, Mexico

States, cities, counties, locales, and addresses:

Nebraska, Boston, Oxfordshire, Brooklyn, Telegraph Hill, 10 Downing Street

Specific buildings, bridges, tunnels, parks, monuments, etc.:

the Empire State Building, the White House, Golden Gate Bridge, Central Park, the Jefferson Memorial, Grand Central Station

Words derived from nations or geographical areas, including all nationalities, ethnicities, and languages:

Asian, Caucasian (White–when used to denote race), Native American, African American (Black–when used to denote race), Hispanic, Arabic, Yoruba, English, Mayan, Nebraskan, Bostonian, Brooklynite

Specific religions and their followers:

Judaism, Jewish, Islam, Muslim, Christianity, Methodist, Buddhist

Institutions, organizations, businesses, departments, etc.:

Cornell University, Elmhurst Hospital, the Library of Congress, the Chamber of Commerce, the American Ballet Theater, the Red Sox

Note: Some organizations are known by their initials; for example: ACLU, AFL, NAACP, NOW, UNICEF. Because these names are **acronyms— where each letter represents a word**—they are completely capitalized. The name of the disease AIDS is also an acronym (see page 18).

Days of the week, months, holidays:

Wednesday, February, Election Day, Groundhog Day

Historical documents:

The Affordable Care Act, The Constitution of The United States of America, The Gettysburg Address, Brown vs. Board of Education, Roe vs. Wade, The Monroe Doctrine

First, last, and all major words in titles and sub-titles of books, articles, songs, on-line documents, etc.

Lead, Follow, or Move Out of the Way: Global Perspectives in Literature and Film.

"Wall Street Heads for a Crash"

punctuation of titles

Italicize or <u>underline</u> the titles of "long" works:

Book-length works, including long poems, plays, films, and TV and radio shows:

The Rise and Fall of the Roman Empire, Alice's Adventures in Wonderland, The Canterbury Tales, A Raisin in the Sun, Star Trek

Periodicals:

The New York Times, Sports Illustrated, The American Journal of Public Health

Full-length musical and artistic creations:

Tchaikovsky's *Concerto for Violin and Orchestra in E minor, Op. 64;* Picasso's *Guernica; Twelve Years a Slave*

Use quotation marks to enclose the titles of "short" writings—essays, articles, stories, short poems, songs, individual episodes of TV and radio shows, etc.

"An Essay on Civil Disobedience," "The Story of an Hour," "Ode to the West Wind," "The Star Spangled Banner," "Self-Reliance"

Use neither italics nor quotation marks for the titles of:

Writings sacred to a religion:

The Bible, the Torah, the Koran, the Upanishads, Ecclesiastes

Documents:

The Magna Carta, the Declaration of Independence, Plessy vs. Ferguson, The Lilly Ledbetter Fair Pay Act

The title of your own piece of writing on your cover sheet or title page.

QUOTATION MARKS (" ")

The main purpose of quotation marks is to **enclose direct quotations** from speech or writing. Quotation marks are always used in pairs, one to <u>open</u> and one to <u>close</u> the quotation.

William Blake wrote that "the road of excess leads to the palace of wisdom."

"Can someone please explain that?" asked the professor.

According to H. D. Thoreau, "most men lead lives of quiet desperation."

Punctuation of Quotations

Periods, commas, and nearly all other punctuation goes inside the quotation marks.

Notice the capitalization, the spacing, and the placement of the commas, the periods, and the question mark in the examples that follow.

Speaker clause first:

Irene Keller smiled and said, "Welcome to our forum."

Quotation first:

"Thank you for inviting me to speak," replied Dr. Moore.

Question mark instead of comma:

"Will you be taking questions from the audience?" Ms. Keller asked.

Two commas when a one-sentence quotation is interrupted by the speaker clause:

"After my lecture," Dr. Moore said, "we can have a question-and-answer period."

One comma and one period for two quoted sentences interrupted by the speaker clause:

"Our guest lecturer is well known to everyone present," announced Ms. Keller. "Today she will be speaking to us about noise pollution."

When the direct quotation is an integral part of the sentence in which it appears, no comma is necessary.

The poet says that "earth's most radiant colors burn through the canvas" of a painting by Rembrandt.

Place colons and semicolons outside quotation marks.

In his card, Mason wrote, "I am so sorry for your loss"; at the funeral, his condolences seemed just as heartfelt.

Put question marks and exclamation points inside quotation marks **unless** they apply to the whole sentence.

Although it seems silly, children often ask, "Do I really have to go to bed?"

Have you heard the saying "Finders keepers"?

Are we really a "country without laws"?

Special Punctuation Inside Quotations

Single quotation marks (' ') enclose a quotation that is inside another quotation.

Gloria Steinem reports that Gandhi "continued to date his life as 'before' and 'after' what he called 'my experiments with truth.'"

Brackets ([ ])

Square brackets contain material inserted into a quotation, either to make the quotation understandable outside of its original context, or to add information. Because the bracket is often used with the ellipsis, it may also be used to assist with the flow of a sentence.

"Her [Johnson's] book claims that they [women]...[should] always remain focused on the rules of law."

or

"[Johnson's] book claims that [women]...[should] always remain focused on the rules of law."

Note: In the second version, the pronouns have been removed. Here, the reader should instantly understand that the writer has provided clarity with the name and gender, and that these nouns have replaced the vague pronouns.

The Latin word *sic* is inserted into a quotation, in brackets, following an error that was made by the author, not by you.

The ad claims that all lite [sic] beer has less calories.

The movie is called The Kids Are Alright *[sic].*

Ellipsis (. . . or . . . .)
Original quotation:

"The woman was happy to oblige the whims of her withered and abusive father before he and his new family moved to Houston. Tomorrow, she and her dad will worship together and embrace the change."

Three dots indicate the omission of a word or words from inside one quoted sentence.

"The woman was happy to oblige her... withered and abusive father before he... moved to Houston."

Four dots indicate that the omission spans more than one sentence. (The fourth dot is the period between the sentences.)

When she confronted her abusive father and he changed his mind, *"The woman was happy to oblige....Tomorrow,...[they] will worship together and embrace the change."*

Note: MLA recommends putting brackets around ellipsis marks.

Note: When using the ellipsis and the bracket, never alter or manipulate the meaning the author intended.

The Block Quote

The Block quote is used for quotations that are four lines or more. For MLA, the quote is double spaced like the rest of the document. It is set off from the main text and indented ten spaces (double tab). Do not use quotation marks. When citing a work, the ending punctuation is now attached to the sentence and not the citation.

It is easy to be opinionated. However, the author argues that many people have totally missed the point:

> Women are not the enemy of men. No, they are the opposite. As a matter of fact, they are the lifeblood that continues to push society forward. As Johnson suggests, 'how can woman be against man? Isn't she his beginning . . . his mother and his wife.' If we are to trust these words . . . [we] must dispel sexist positioning and embrace a unified humanity. If not, all will be lost. (Shannon 29)

Other Uses of Quotation Marks

To indicate the title of a short work—poem, article, story, etc.

"Song of Myself"

To cast doubt on the sincerity of a word.

Your "friend" has just stolen your car.

numbers

Spell out numbers that are written in one or two words.

Five   twenty-nine   seventy

Use numerals for numbers that are written in three or more words.

2,339   142

Spell out numbers that begin a sentence.

Eight hundred seven years ago, a man fell off a horse.

He owns 807 horses.

Use numerals for dates, page references, fractions, decimals, percentages, scores, statistics, and surveys.

June 14th, 2008	*Page 5*	*1/2*
0.032	*99.9% pure*	*7 to 13, 21–12*
Average age 18	*6 out of 10 dentists recommend*	

Use numerals for a list or series of numbers.

23, 45, 67, 89

Use numerals for exact times.

2:13 p.m.

Use numerals for papers on scientific or technical subjects.

The area of our given metallic object is $49.71 \pm 0.19 \ cm^2$.

1 2 3 **4** 5

The Writing Process

"I don't want to do it." "Why?" "Borrrring." If you are a student writer, these thoughts, among others, occurred to you the moment you were given an essay prompt and the corresponding due date. Only those who have a true affinity for books and writing get a warm fuzzy feeling when they are presented with a writing prompt or assignment. Why? For many student writers, academic writing inspires dread, fear, and anxiety; so much so, students often postpone writing much to their own detriment. Unless a student is truly excited about studying with a specific instructor, the course/course content, or the assignment, it is very difficult to feel good about writing.

Undeniably, there is much for the student writer to contemplate: deciphering the essay topic, pre-writing, writing, the gathering of sources, pre-grade anxiety, and post-grade depression. Additionally, should the instructor take pity upon the writer, the student may still struggle with how best to improve the paper during the revision process. Now, the student writer must consider all that was done before, make improvements, and decipher the instructor's comments scribbled throughout the paper.

Writing an essay is not an instantaneous act. It is a process that must evolve over time. Besides writing, you must consider what you are up against: what is being asked of you, your intention(s) as a writer, the deadline/due date, use of primary and secondary sources, and the length of the assignment. Whether you believe it or not, your instructor knows what you are going through, and s/he is there to aid you as you navigate the writing process. As such, use this knowledge to your advantage. Meet with your instructor as soon as you receive the assignment. If drafting is not already a part of the assignment, ask the instructor if you are allowed to submit a working version of the paper before the due date. If at all possible, work with a tutor. DO NOT WRITE without consulting a proofreader (instructor, tutor, trusted peer), and, most important, DO NOT wait until the last minute.

Moreover, knowing the rules of grammar and having a strong vocabulary are only part of what it means to be a good writer. While it is essential to "know the rules" and utilize language well, having something to say and saying it effectively are skills that also need to be developed. Often, however, student essays lack substance and focus. This chapter will show you how to begin, develop, and conclude an essay worth reading.

where students go wrong

You have been given an assignment and a due date for that assignment. If you are lucky, the instructor has provided you with a detailed list of expectations and parameters for the paper. You take notes. You nod. You understand. **But do you really get it?**

In the previous section, we've attempted to give you some helpful "getting started" hints, but there are others. As such, before you put pen to paper or anxious fingertips to a clicking keyboard, the following should be done:

- See the instructor immediately after the essay is assigned. During this meeting, make sure that **what** you think you heard is the same as what was **said**.
- Determine whether or not you must adhere to the essay prompt or if it is an **open** topic that will allow you to have your own creative spin on the subject matter.
- Ask whether or not you will be required to use both primary and secondary sources.
- Ask whether or not you will be allowed to write in First Person.
- Be clear about the essay's due date and if a revision is possible should the first attempt be less than successful.
- When possible, form study/writing groups. These kinds of groups serve as support systems for struggling writers and can also help to keep you on schedule.
- Make sure that style manual and all stylistic requirements—font, margins, spacing, citations—are understood before you begin writing.

types of essays

The Basic Five Paragraph Essay (Expository Essay)

The structure of the basic essay is quite simple. It includes the following:

- An introductory paragraph that includes a provable thesis statement.

- Three body paragraphs. Each paragraph should include a thesis-related topic sentence and supporting evidence to analyze, support, and defend your ideas and claims.

- A conclusion that wraps up your thoughts.

THE FOUNDATION:

As a new student in your first college writing class, consider utilizing a five paragraph outline for your first set of essays. Many essays, of course, are much longer, but even longer essays follow this basic structure.

Paragraph one: *The Introduction*

Your introductory paragraph should include the following elements: *A hook:* Your writing should immediately draw your reader in. Consider beginning your introduction with a startling fact, a question, a quote, or a short anecdote (i.e., story) that leads your reader to your topic. *Background information* (*Informational Development*): Provide just the right amount of information necessary for your reader to understand your topic. *Thesis statement:* This is where you make the topic and purpose of your paper clear. It also provides an overview of the main supporting points you will be covering. The thesis statement usually appears in the last sentence. If you are writing in response to one or more readings, the introductions should include the title of the piece, the author's full name, and the type of writing it is (essay, article, story, poem, etc.). In your discussion of articles and stories, be sure to write in the present tense (see informational development on pages 81-82).

Paragraph Two: *Body Paragraph*

Begin with a *topic sentence* that establishes the single main idea that will be discussed in support of your thesis statement. (see topic sentence on page 83) Your supporting sentences should include specific details, examples, and quotes that serve to expand on the main idea. Be sure to introduce your quotes with signal phrases and to comment on quotes after using them. (see signal phrase on page 84). Be sure all your sentences relate directly to the main idea. If you move on to a new idea, make a new paragraph.

Paragraph Three: *Body Paragraph*

Again, begin with a *topic sentence* that signals that a new point is being introduced. Your supporting sentences should include specific details, examples, and quotes that serve to expand on the main idea. Use *transition words or phrases* to move from sentences *within* your paragraph and from one paragraph to the next.

Paragraph Four: *Body Paragraph*

Begin this paragraph with the final *topic sentence* that relates back to the remaining point mentioned in the thesis statement. Again, provide support, maintain paragraph unity, and transition fluidly.

Paragraph Five: *Conclusion*

Unless asked to summarize, the conclusion does not restate, revisit, or rehash what has been said in previous paragraphs. The purpose of the conclusion is to conclude. It is your final opportunity to explain to the reader why your argument matters. Ultimately, this paragraph, referring to the previous paragraphs, says " I just told you all of this information because this is the point I want you to understand."

the extended essay
(beyond expository essay writing)

Advanced Composition and Literature Courses

Once you move beyond the basic essay (expository writing) and progress as a writer, the content of your assigned writing projects will change drastically. Including primary and secondary sources to support or defend your claims will become a necessary part of writing. You will be asked to write longer papers, and, while the instructor is attempting to ferret out your feelings about a text or course content, unlike the basic essay, these are NOT "tell me how you feel" papers. Instead, the instructor may ask you to critically analyze and assess a text, explore the similarities between texts, discuss authorial intent, analyze a concept, or argue a position or alternative. Moreover, you will be asked to do all of this and more without using the first person "I."

Advanced writers must be critical readers, writers, and researchers. When you are asked to write a critical essay or literary criticism, you are NOT being asked to be negative. Instead, you are being asked to be discerning: original, thoughtful, careful, analytical, and innovative as a writer. Advanced writing is not a book report. On the contrary, it is you at your best taking a new and interesting approach to the assigned material.

STRUCTURE OF THE ADVANCED ESSAY

The basic structure of all essays is the same:

- Interesting introduction with a provable thesis.
- A series of body paragraphs that include thesis-related topic sentences supported with examples (quotes) from supporting texts to defend your claims/assertions.
- Transitions within sentences and between body paragraphs. (see documenting sources page 107)
- Concluding remarks that wrap up the essay as interestingly as you began it.
- Proper use of grammar and vocabulary.

Note: Do not panic as you transition from the basic essay to advanced/extended essay writing. You are simply doing more of the same. Introductions and body paragraphs may become longer. Thesis statements are much more specific and, sometimes, longer. Supporting evidence may come from multiple sources. The extended essay (advanced writing) is simply more of what you have already learned to do.

WRITING WHEN PROMPTED

The wonderful thing about the extended essay (advanced writing) is that, quite often, the instructor may design the research topic or essay prompt as a way of guiding you through the writing process. The essay or writing prompt is a useful tool as it allows you to remain focused. Without focus, your paper does not stand a chance. While having a prompt makes writing easier in many ways, there are still guidelines that you must follow in order to write effectively: you **must** determine what type of prompt you're working with, and you **must** do some freewriting before you submit your paper.

CLOSED AND OPEN ESSAY PROMPTS:

Closed: There is an assigned topic or task. The instructor has laid out a clear path to a successful essay. The instructor has asked you to respond to a specific question and has asked you to take specific ideas into consideration as you formulate your response.

Example: *Toni Morrison's novel* Paradise *is a multi-faceted text that spans the creation and demise of the fictional town of Ruby in the state of Oklahoma. By focusing on a single community whose inhabitants rarely change, the author is able to explore, in detail, the elements of race, gender, and violence and the way(s) in which they are interrelated. Discuss in detail how this is true. Also, using at least one of the fictional Ruby families as a means of supporting your argument, explore the family's awkwardness or ignorance as they are confronted with issues of race or gender bias. Additionally, explore why the use of violence or force becomes the norm when members of the family or the family as a whole are confronted with change as it relates to race and gender. You must use specific examples from the text to support your claims. Secondary sources written by critics of Morrison's work should be used. The paper must be 5–7 pages long, must have a Works Cited page, and use MLA format. It is due on April 16th. Late papers will not be accepted.*

Open: The topic/focal point are fixed, but the instructor allows you to construct your own response to the essay prompt. Additionally, an open essay prompt may allow you to construct both the subject matter and the evolution of the essay.

Example: *Write a paper about Toni Morrison's novel <u>Paradise</u>. During our class discussions, we determined that the novel addresses everything from slavery to mass murder; as such, you have many topics to choose from. The paper should discuss a moment in the text that impacted you on a visceral level; so much so, it begs further exploration and discussion. Please use specific examples from the text to support your ideas. Secondary sources would be nice but are not required. You may also use personal examples from your own life as a means of defending your idea(s).*

freewriting

A good way to get ideas about a topic is to **freewrite**. You can respond to a text you have just read or to an assigned topic. In freewriting, write continuously without a plan for ten or twenty minutes. Don't worry about grammar, spelling, or organization. Just write. Once you are finished, go back to what you have written and highlight the essential points that you have developed. Look for recurring themes or a premise that appears to be revealing itself. Let these indicators determine your focus for a larger essay.

When you are assigned an essay, you may believe that your instructor simply wants you to repackage classroom discussions. This is not true. Any good instructor wants to know what you think and why you feel the way you do. They also want you to support your findings. Consider this, you may be one of twenty-five students in a given class. Why would any reader want to re-read the same paper twenty-five times? While the subject matter may be the same, the instructor is looking for an interesting or insightful observation from a student who is invested in the text or topic. As there is much at stake for both the reader and the writer, all essay writing should begin with a freewrite. Your freewrite can be a tentative outline of how you would like to proceed or a few pages of unedited writing.

Example of Closed Essay Prompt FreeWrite

Essay on Morrison

race

all black town formed by freed slaves → population does not allow/ tolerate mixing of the races → inhabitants do not allow interaction with Blacks whose racial "purity" has been compromised.

gender

strong women	*vs.*	*weak women*
women who live in the convent who are not native to Ruby (Connie, Mavis, Pallas, Grace, Seneca)		most of the women from Ruby; especially Soane and Dovey Morgan

from the town of Ruby → Billie Delia

violence

men of Ruby murder male outsiders who propositioned Ruby women → KD Morgan slaps Arnette when she demands that he deal with their unplanned teen pregnancy → Ruby townspeople ostracize Billie Delia because they believe her to be promiscuous, and her mother attacks her → the men of Ruby, led by the Morgans, set out to murder the women of the convent because they believe them to be "unclean."

Primary Family Focus → The Morgans

This outline responds directly to the instructor's questions within the essay prompt. It also highlights specific moments from the text that can support the writer's claims; moreover, it will keep the writer on topic.

constructing the thesis statement

Once you have fleshed out what you want to write about, you will need to construct a solid and provable thesis statement. Without a thesis, you **DO NOT** have a paper. **Developing a thesis statement is very difficult, but it gets easier once you master the concept.** Simply put, the thesis is what you want to write about or what you are going to prove. This chapter will refer to the thesis several times because it is THAT important. If you do not have a thesis, you do not have a paper—period. The thesis anchors the paper and helps you to construct your topic sentences, as well as develop strong body paragraphs.

Let's use Toni Morrison's *Paradise* once again. Here, we will use the **Open** Essay Prompt as we construct a workable Thesis Statement. In this case, the prompt simply asks that the writer choose a specific theme and write about its importance or significance. In other words, student writers should choose a theme that impacted them—grabbed their attention—while reading.

If the student is lucky, there will be no problem choosing a theme. However, most students are not that lucky.

Example Open Essay Prompt on Morrison's *Paradise* (theme choice)

Lucky Student: Violence and the lack of personal knowledge in Morrison's *Paradise*

Unlucky Student: I hated this book. Why did we read this?

The Lucky Student may have a **topic** for discussion, but there is **no** thesis.

The Unlucky Student does not have a topic, yet there is a way to turn a negative into a positive.

HOW TO DO IT:

Lucky must ask some basic questions:

Who uses violence?	The Men of Ruby
What kind of violence?	Threats, Yelling, Fights, Domestic Abuse, Murder
When specifically is the violence used?	When confronted about their decision making
What is personal knowledge?	Acceptance of the changing world and the ideas of others
Why is the personal knowledge unattainable?	They isolate themselves
Why?	They want the town to remain pure and unchanged

Lucky may want to use this as a thesis: People in Ruby use violence because they lack personal knowledge.

BUT, Lucky should use the following instead: In Toni Morrison's novel *Paradise,* the men of Ruby, Oklahoma use violent tactics such as yelling, intimidation, and murder as a means of protecting their *seemingly* safe and isolated world from change and new ideas.

Unlucky must ask the following:

Why do I *hate* this book?	Because it rehashes old ideas
What do I mean by this?	We don't have slaves anymore, and women have equal rights
What else don't I like about the book?	It's way too violent
Why is this a problem?	It's overkill. I was so focused on the violence that I stopped paying attention to the so-called issues

Unlucky may want to use the following as a thesis: Toni Morrison's *Paradise* is out-of-date and way too violent.

Unlucky should use this one instead: Toni Morrison's novel *Paradise* fails to connect with the contemporary reader because it rehashes antiquated social issues that have long-since been resolved; additionally, the text examines these social issues against a very violent backdrop that makes it almost impossible to focus on the relevant problems presented.

Note: All student writers should consider these two things:

1. Very rarely is your first attempt at a thesis the best one. A thesis should be able to withstand the **SO WHAT?** question. Look at the first attempts for Lucky and Unlucky. Each attempt lacks specificity. In short, the reader will have more questions after s/he encounters it, and the writer will surely have trouble constructing a well-developed essay around it. Therefore, after you have written your thesis, ask *so what?*

2. It is possible to construct a thesis and develop an essay that you feel good about even when you are less than enthusiastic about the text.

organizing advanced essay writing

There are several different approaches to developing a well-written and concise essay. Unfortunately, many students have the same complaints when it comes to their writing: I don't know where to start; I'm not sure what I want to say; I run out of things to say; I find that I frequently repeat myself.

Because of these typical writing issues, many writers find that they lose focus as the essay unfolds; moreover, they complain that their thinking is jumbled and that their paragraphs lack cohesion. In order to make an essay your own and not just something you are trying to submit for a grade, the mapping out of the essay should be approached more succinctly. As such, the goal is to develop writing that says what you want it to say and, at the same time, presents the instructor with a "reader-friendly" essay that establishes a position, defends it, and concludes just as strongly as it began.

Your objective is to present yourself on paper in a manner that shows that you understand the topic or literature and are capable of insightful thinking that does not regurgitate material. Unless assigned, the **book report style of writing** should be avoided. We have designed two organizational formats: The Chart and the Scaffolding Format. Both are designed to aide you as you construct your essay, help you to stay focused (stick to your thesis), incorporate sources, and establish an argument that is entirely yours.

The Chart

To avoid the pitfalls of writing—not having enough to say, not knowing how to start, lack of focus, lack of substance, redundancy—we recommend using an organizational system known as "The Chart." As you will come to understand, the elements of "The Chart" will help determine the major components of your essay, including your introductory, body, and concluding paragraphs.

To begin strategizing your essay, establish the following elements:

The Topic

Whether your own, assigned, or discerned from comprehending some form of literature, a main idea always exists. What is your paper's main idea?

The Focus

What are you trying to explore regarding your topic? This understanding is the aspect of the topic that you will look at concisely.

The Purpose

There are several options to consider when establishing the reason you are writing your essay: do you wish to argue a point, to entertain, to inform, to persuade, to dissuade, to educate, to reveal, to analyze, to explain, to describe, or to compare? All papers must have a specific intention in mind or the document will never take an effective form. Without purpose, the writer is merely typing.

The Audience

The group you have in mind as you develop your paper's position. Rarely, if ever, will a student write a paper for him/herself. You, the writer, must consider a group that you want to address or who you specifically want to read your essay. What group are you developing your paper's ideas for: teenagers, politicians, college students, scholars in a specific field, single mothers between eighteen and thirty-five years old?

Tone

How you speak to your reader. What is the voice you want to project: angry, disappointed, aggressive, concerned, sarcastic, ashamed? Tone is essential for developing the language of the essay. Understanding how you feel about the paper's topic will allow you to establish your own voice as a writer. Once understood, tone literally determines the words used to develop sentences.

Attending to these elements of "The Chart" will make your writing process highly focused. You can now advance to preparing your thesis statement; however, without additional fine tuning you run the risk of still having holes in your paper. We recommend implementing the 5 "W's" to give your work greater substance. Without including the 5 "W's," your reader may misunderstand or question your paper's argument.

The 5 "W's"

Who: the subject matter of the topic and focus (does not have to be a person)

What: literally "what" your subject matter is about

Why: the issue/problem (the why always answers the what)

When: the time frame of the issue

Where: the location of the issue/problem

When developing the chart, only use between one and three words. The more succinct "The Chart" is, the less of a chance there is for developmental confusion. Also, keep in mind that the reason for developing "The Chart" is to provide a map that contains all of the basic elements of the paper; as such, nothing on "The Chart" ever repeats.

Observe the following examples.

Example One

Topic: Animals	**Who** (subject matter): Dog Fighting
Focus: Cruelty	**What** (what about dog fighting will you address?): prevalent
Purpose: Persuade	**Why** (why is it prevalent?): weak legislation
Audience: Lawmakers	**When:** currently
Tone: Angry	**Where:** southern states

After cultivating the divisions of the paper in the chart, test its effectiveness by either saying aloud or writing "The Chart" out into a statement.

Resulting Paper Proposal

In an angry voice speaking to lawmakers, I will attempt to persuade them to push for stronger laws preventing cruelty to animals. My subject matter is dog fighting. I will show that this inhumane practice is prevalent because of weak legislation that currently exists in southern states.

Example Two

Topic: Bedford-Stuyvesant	**Who** (subject matter): Architecture
Focus: Hidden Pleasures	**What:** Magnificent
Purpose: Persuade	**Why:** Craftmanship
Audience: Non-residents	**When:** 19th Century
Tone: Encouraging	**Where:** Myrtle Avenue

Resulting Paper Proposal

In an encouraging voice speaking to non-residents, I will attempt to persuade them about the hidden pleasures of Bedford-Stuyvesant. I will show that the architecture on Myrtle Avenue is magnificent due to exquisite nineteenth-century craftsmanship.

Example Three (Text-Related Topic)

This example is based on a text-based reading of the novella *Krik? Krak!* The only difference between this example and the first two is that all the elements of "The Chart" will draw from the published work at hand.

Text: Edwidge Danticat's *Krik? Krak!*

Topic: Mothers and daughters   **Who** (subject matter): Storytelling

Focus: Bonding   **What:** evokes memories

Purpose: Analyze   **Why:** remind

Audience: College students   **When:** present and past

Tone: Sympathetic   **Where:** Haiti/Brooklyn

Resulting Paper Proposal

In a sympathetic voice speaking to college students, I will analyze the bonding between mothers and daughters in Edwidge Danticat's *Krik? Krak!* I will show how the subject matter of storytelling is used to evoke memories in an attempt to remind younger Haitians living in Brooklyn of their historical identity.

Note: One of the key components of effective writing is the thinking process. "The Chart" allows the writer to actually outline the paper's needs completely, providing you with the opportunity to actually step away from the work and return without losing any understanding. Once understood, the chart eliminates almost all developmental problems regarding essay writing.

Note: The paper proposal is a mini-abstract. (see page 98)

three-pronged thesis statement

It is now time to clarify the argument of your paper, also known as the thesis statement. One of the best ways to develop a working thesis is to come up with three specific points that will prove the proposal developed using "The Chart." This style of thesis is the most comprehensive way of developing the essay's body structure. In the first example about animal cruelty, come up with three prongs—points—that your essay will prove regarding the paper proposal. For example, the three points that you will need to address to persuade lawmakers to strengthen animal cruelty laws in southern states are (1) that animal cruelty damages the animals involved, (2) that stiffer penalties are needed, and (3) the impounding of material possessions would serve as the most severe deterrent.

Now put this into a sentence.

Here, we have a basic thesis statement that contains the three prongs:

Clearly, dog fighting is damaging to the animals involved, and many southern states must recognize the need for new laws that increase jail sentences and, most stringently, repossess the property of offenders.

Below we have the same thesis sentence which includes more of the grammatical elements discussed in **Chapter 2**. The objective over time is to be able to make the thesis more sophisticated and, inevitably, make the paper more sophisticated.

Clearly, dog fighting, a barbaric event pitting innocent canines in a fight to the death, is severely damaging to animals; as such, many southern states must recognize that unless new laws are established–increasing jail sentences and repossessing property–these horrendous acts will continue unchecked.

THE SCAFFOLDING FORMAT

The Chart is one way of formulating structure within your extended essay or research paper. The Scaffolding Format is another. Scaffolding ensures that you adhere to the essay basics, attribute your sources properly, and construct equally strong opening and closing remarks.

I. The Introduction

The introduction of a paper is the initial opportunity to grab the reader's interest and establish your argument. It is, in essence, the one opportunity to present your position to your readers and to captivate them with your writing.

There are a variety of ways to begin an essay, but here are three ways that work well:

The Question

The Quote

The Anecdote

THE QUESTION

At the beginning of your essay, pose a thought-provoking question to your readers that engages them and fosters thought on the subject matter.

An opening question for an essay on providing equal opportunities for women may look something like this:

Historically, women have been making the argument for equal treatment under the law in business and in their households, but at what point will society finally strip away their status as second-class citizens?

THE QUOTE

A worthwhile trick of the trade is to use a well-known and respected person's words to help introduce your ideas and then segue into the conversation that will take place within your essay.

For example, a paper on the midlife crisis experience in America might begin this way:

"The mass of men lead lives of quiet desperation." These words, written by essayist and philosopher Henry David Thoreau, speak to the deep sadness that many experience once they turn forty–often considered the autumn of one's life.

In this case, the words and ideas immediately following the famous quote belong to you.

THE ANECDOTE

An anecdote allows you to take a piece of life—the world around you, if you will—and apply it in short story form to your paper. The anecdote must speak directly to the idea you're trying to convey in your essay.

For example, the same paper on the midlife crisis might begin this way when using an anecdote:

As a child, I often marveled at the love my father expressed for us on a daily basis. He seemed to deeply adore my mother and doted on us to no end. Quite often, the neighbors would remark how before entering our home, he'd sit for a few minutes watching his beloved family through our large picture frame window, which peered into the living room. Dad never spoke of these moments until much later in life, when I had a wife and child of my own. One day he said to me, "Now you will understand what I went through for so many years. Everyday, I sat in our driveway before entering the house, wondering if I'd made the right decision about being a husband and father. One time, I almost backed the car away and drove off into another life."

INFORMATIONAL DEVELOPMENT

Once you have decided upon an opening, you will need an additional set of ideas that will further your argument and then eventually lead directly to your thesis statement. This is called **informational development**. Informational development is a series of sentences that begin a general discussion about your paper's topic/theme.

For example, using the same paper topic on the American midlife crisis, the informational development might look something like this:

So much of our environment focuses on the individual's quest for happiness. Indeed, almost all facets of our life–faith, politics, and popular culture–speak to the promise and the pursuit of happiness. But, upon further examination of the human life, we appear to be less happy and deeply dissatisfied with who and what we are. These feelings appear to become even more pronounced as we grow older, believing that there is little time to right the things that have gone wrong in our lives.

Here you see that the **informational development** should be connected to the ideas expressed in your opening lines and should, of course, flow seamlessly into your thesis statement.

THESIS STATEMENT

You have already learned how to construct a well-written thesis statement that presents a specific position. Should you have any remaining questions about the construction of the thesis statement, please refer back to pages 73-75.

Here is a sample **thesis statement** on the midlife crisis:

Indeed, the midlife crisis is not a new phenomena in this country, but it is the cause of the disintegration of many American families, and, because it destroys the perception of who we are and impacts how we treat others, we must get to the root of its causes and, ultimately, destroy this great destroyer of American families.

THE FINAL PRODUCT

If you put all of the elements together, the final product looks like this:

"The mass of men lead lives of quiet desperation." These words, written by essayist and philosopher Henry David Thoreau, speak to the deep sadness that many experience once they turn forty–often considered the autumn of one's life. So much of our environment focuses on the individual's quest for happiness. Indeed, almost all facets of our life–faith, politics, and popular culture–speak to the promise and the pursuit of happiness. But, upon further examination of human life, we appear to be less happy and deeply dissatisfied with who and what we are. These feelings appear to become even more pronounced as we grow older, believing that there is little time to right the things that have gone wrong in our lives. Indeed, the midlife crisis is not a new phenomena in this country, but it is the cause of the disintegration of many American families, and, because it destroys the perception of who we are and impacts how we treat others, we

must get to the root of its causes and, ultimately, destroy this great destroyer of American families.

Note: Let's examine the introduction:

Topic = Midlife crisis

Focus = Dissatisfaction

and 5 "W's"

Who: Ill feelings

What: More pronounced

Why: Aging

When: At 40

Where: America

In America, the midlife crisis causes ill feelings that become more pronounced with age, especially when one turns forty.

II. body paragraphs

Everything has a formula, especially your body paragraphs. Consider that your body paragraphs are layered, much like a sandwich, each element or layer adding to the texture and flavor of your essay.

Body Paragraph Elements:

The Topic Sentence

Explanation of the Topic Sentence

Signal Phrase

Support of the Explanation or Use of Quote

Note on the quote (if applicable)

The Transition/Wrap-up Sentence

Let's continue with the theme of the midlife crisis and see if we can develop a strong body paragraph using "the elements."

A. TOPIC SENTENCE

The **topic sentence** is very closely connected to the thesis statement. If the thesis statement governs the paper, topic sentences govern the paragraphs. In fact, the paragraph's topic sentence largely reflects the prong(s) from your thesis statement. The purpose of the **topic**

sentence is twofold: it prevents the overloading of the paragraph with information, and, at the same time, it allows writers to be specific and concise without veering off topic.

If we take one of the prongs from the thesis we constructed earlier, we may have a topic sentence that looks like this:

The American midlife crisis affects both genders and somehow distorts the individual's perception of who they are and their respective lots in life.

Note: Nothing will be included in this paragraph that does not speak directly to this statement.

B. EXPLANATION

Explanation of the topic sentence: What is needed now is a series of ideas—in your own words—that explain specifically what you meant by the sentiments expressed in your topic sentence:

In essence, those who are in the midst of a midlife crisis do not see the reality of their lives. Instead, they see a distorted image of the lives they've lived thus far. Their mate may seem less ideal than the spouse they imagined they could have had. Their place of business may feel more like a job than the career they so desperately believed they would always find engaging. Moreover, they may have the sense that there are more years behind them than in front of them.

As you can see, the **explanation of the topic sentence** further illustrates or expands upon the initial idea(s) established in your topic sentence. It should be specific and lead into introducing an outside source that will support your argument.

C. SIGNAL PHRASE

The **signal phrase** tells the reader that the forthcoming statement belongs to someone else (see page 104).

For the midlife crisis example, the **signal phrase** could look like this:

According to Dr. Diana Patino, author of "It Ain't Over Yet: A Re-examination of the Middle Passage of Life,"

The **signal phrase** should then be combined with the author's quote:

According to Dr. Diana Patino's "It Ain't Over Yet: A Re-examination of the Middle Passage of Life,"

> *Both men and women are subject to the midlife crisis because of environmental factors. Those who experience it do not have to be*

pre-disposed to depression or other substantial mental conflict. For these individuals, life has no surprises left, and they are fearful that their talent and aspirations exceeds what life will allow them to accomplish. The solution is to get the individual to re-visualize their perception of their past, present, and future by giving them a new ruler of measurement that defines personal success. (67)

Note: It is important that your chosen quote isn't merely something you like. Rather, the chosen quote should connect to the topic sentence. In doing so, it further supports and defends your thesis statement.

D. QUOTING

Quoting: The chapter on conducting research and putting together an actual research paper will give a more in-depth discussion about the varied ways you can use the ideas expressed in an essay, article, short story, poem, or novel to support a given argument. As you will discover, in the following chapter, different disciplines use distinct styles for incorporating supporting evidence and putting together the "Works Cited" page.

For the sake of our paper, let's use the basic format for in-text quoting using MLA documentation. Because the paper attempts to take a position about the midlife crisis that appears to need evidence that can be supported by medical or psychological experts or perhaps even essays/articles written by those who have experienced the condition, the paper will need to be reinforced by an expert in the field who fulfills one of the aforementioned categories.

For this essay, we have a psychologist who has counseled men and women who suffer from the midlife crisis. She has also written extensively on the issue for medical journals. This person is a valid and credible source because of her expertise and credentials. Her ideas, therefore, should be used to support the ideas expressed in your paper and, moreover, her words support/defend the thesis statement.

The previous section, on the **Signal Phrase**, shows how best to insert a basic in-text quote into your body paragraph.

E. NOTE ON THE QUOTE

The next step in designing a paragraph is called the **note on the quote**. Here, the writer explains the significance of the quote and the way that it reinforces the ideas put forth in the **topic sentence**:

Although Dr. Patino cautions that the midlife crisis is commonplace, it is clear that the individual need not have any pre-existing conditions, which may cause a great sigh of relief for some who worry that this sudden sadness is something more serious. At the same time, there appears to be hope for those who find their lives in a so-called stalemate; these individuals can, in fact, re-imagine themselves. Dr. Patino also goes a long way in unearthing the taboos of growing old, positioning the crisis as all too real and not as something that makes men and women of a certain age color their hair and buy sports cars.

It should be noted that the **note on the quote** need not always be positive.

Note: quotes serve the purpose of the writer. So you may disagree with the quote if it fails to make an idea clear or leaves out a pertinent point.

F. TRANSITION SENTENCE

Finally, the last part of a paragraph is the **transition sentence**. The **transition sentence** both wraps up your paragraph and sets up what's to come in the next body paragraph:

While Dr. Patino makes the suggestion that the midlife crisis is separate from pre-existing medical conditions, there are those who believe that her assertion is flawed.

Here you see that the aforementioned sentence sets up a new topic sentence that will address the flipside to Dr. Patino's position.

Now that you have witnessed the paragraph process, let's examine how it works when the pieces are put together.

SAMPLE BODY PARAGRAPH

The American midlife crisis affects both genders and somehow distorts the individual's perception of who they are and their respective lots in life. In essence, those who are in the midst of a midlife crisis do not see the reality of their lives. Instead, they see a distorted image of the life they've lived thus far. Their mate may seem less ideal than the spouse they imagined they could have had. Their place of business may feel more like a job than the career they so desperately believed they would always find engaging. Moreover, they may have the sense that there are more years behind them than in front of them. According to Dr. Diana Patino's "It Ain't Over Yet: A re-examination of the Middle Passage of Life,"

> *Both men and women are subject to the midlife crisis because of environmental factors. Those who experience it do not have to be pre-disposed to depression or other substantial mental conflict. For these individuals, life has no surprises left, and they are fearful that their talent and aspirations exceed what life will allow them to accomplish.*

The solution is to get the individual to re-visualize their perception of their past, present, and future by giving them a new ruler of measurement that defines personal success. (67)

Although Dr. Patino cautions that the midlife crisis is commonplace, it is clear that the individual need not have any pre-existing conditions, which may cause a great sigh of relief for some who worry that this sudden sadness is something more serious. At the same time, there appears to be hope for those who find their lives in a so-called stalemate; these individuals can, in fact, re-imagine themselves. Dr. Patino also goes a long way in unearthing the taboos of growing old, positioning the crisis as all too real and not as something that makes men and women of a certain age color their hair and buy sports cars. While Dr. Patino makes the suggestion that the midlife crisis is separate from pre-existing medical conditions, there are those who believe that her assertion is flawed.

Following this format will go a long way in allowing you to present strong, well-written, and properly supported paragraphs to your reader.

the conclusion

For some, writing the conclusion is the most difficult part of the essay. Often, the internal question the writer is plagued with is, "what can I say that I haven't already said?"

Imagine your concluding paragraph(s) this way: what if you sat in a movie theater watching the best movie ever and then for the remaining thirty minutes it literally restated everything you had viewed for ninety minutes? Quite naturally, you would be confused and dismayed and have no real sense of what the point was. You would probably be so offended that you would want your money back.

The same holds true for concluding paragraphs. You do not want to run the risk of having your readers feel as if they were short-changed by having no real finalization of your point.

Revisiting "The Chart," **the conclusion** includes your **purpose, audience, and tone**. It is not a place for the writer to reiterate or restate ideas that you have spent several pages presenting to the reader. In essence, just as the introduction introduces, the goal of the conclusion is to conclude:

The midlife crisis is real. More importantly, it is a crisis that millions of Americans experience and, very soon, we may find ourselves among the numbers who suffer from the condition. What those of us, individuals who have yet to turn forty, need to know is that despite how technologically savvy we have become with our inventions, how advanced we have become in our ideas on class, race, or gender, no matter how ever-evolving the bodies that govern us become, we are still prone to the whims of our physical selves and minds. And when either entity tells us to stop, reevaluate our lives, or that we are sad, we can do no more than listen wholeheartedly. Perhaps the so-called midlife crisis would lose some of its stigma if we regarded it not as the passage of time—the onslaught of old age—but as a time to welcome that which is yet to come. Moreover, it should be viewed as the moment when we become the best of who we are and strengthen the ideas that have brought us thus far.

Note: Let's examine the conclusion:

Purpose = to prepare

Audience = 30-somethings

Tone = hopeful

In a hopeful voice, speaking to 30-somethings, this essay will prepare them for the stigmas that often accompany turning forty.

titling an original essay

All written texts, regardless of topic, genre, or discipline—e.g., Rome, sexuality, love, essay, poem, research paper, thesis, dissertation, English, art, or psychology classes—should always have an original title. The title should be a reflection of what the writing conveys to the reader. Beyond being the introduction to the work, it piques the reader's interest and inspires them to continue reading.

Chasing True Love in an eHarmony World.

For critical essays that examine a specific literary text, the examined writing cannot be the title, but it may be a part of the title.

Looking in the Garden: Examining Space and Place in Sarah Gordon's "Where the Hungry Girls Live."

patterns of organization

The way you construct your thesis statement will ultimately determine your writing pattern. There are four writing patterns: chronological, emphatic, simple to complex, and spatial.

CHRONOLOGICAL PATTERN

An essay that follows the **chronological pattern** will be ordered according to the sequence in which events occur. For example, a paper on women's rights in America might begin with the Seneca Falls Convention of 1848, then discuss the passage of the Women's Right to Vote in 1920, and end with the Women's Liberation Movement of the 1960s.

EMPHATIC WRITING PATTERN

An essay that follows the **emphatic writing pattern** is organized according to emphasis, or importance, of the developing points. The most important point will either be introduced first or will appear last depending on the writer's preference. Perhaps you want your strongest point to hit the reader immediately. Alternately, you might save the strongest point until last, leaving your reader with a lasting impression.

Let's look at a paper that examines the best deterrents for the crime of murder. This paper will be developed around these three prongs: the death penalty, a moral society, and gun control. Now, look at these two sample thesis sentences.

This thesis statement places the emphasis in the beginning of the sentence:

The death penalty is the most effective way to deter the crime of murder in a society; teaching social morality is another decent argument for deterrence, but we should also keep in mind effective gun control.

This thesis sentence places emphasis at the end of the sentence:

Many argue that the death penalty is a frightening deterrent to murder, yet a more effective method is to promote morality in schools; without effective gun control, however, neither one of these methods proves successful.

SIMPLE TO COMPLEX

Simple to Complex as a pattern says that the ordering lists the most simplistic factor first and builds to the most complex. **When writing an essay, freewriting is the simplest act. Outlining is the next stage and requires more thought. Finally, constructing the body of the essay is the most complicated stage.**

SPATIAL

Spatial examines writing from a concept of space. If you were writing a paper describing a classroom, the discussion would be based on the writer's positioning in the room. If located in the back of the room on the left hand side, the entire writing would be based on this location. At the same time, spatial also discusses perspective.If writing a paper on women's rights, a spatial perspective develops when you examine the subject matter from a Black woman's, a White woman's, or an Asian woman's point of view.

Note: These patterns may often overlap, but one will generally dominate.

writing forms

One of the most helpful ways to develop paragraphs and, for that matter, whole essays is to understand the way in which your argument, whatever it may be, will develop. This stage is where understanding the functions of the various writing forms come into play. There are essentially ten writing forms to choose from. These patterns are ways in which our thinking organizes itself on the page. Keep in mind that the more sophisticated your writing becomes, the more these forms, similar to the patterns, will overlap.

DESCRIPTION

Sketches portraits of a person, place, or thing by using specific details.

NARRATION

Tells a story or part of a story. These paragraphs are usually chronological, but they may also contain flashbacks.

COMPARISON AND CONTRAST

To compare two subjects is to establish a connection to similarities; however, comparing often provides a consideration of differences. To contrast only points out differences.

ARGUMENTATIVE

Although all essays are to varying degrees argumentative, an essay or paragraph that addresses a specific argument or debate will establish the debate, take a position within the debate, and often consider counter-arguments to the debate.

DEFINITION

A definition puts an idea or term into a general class and then provides enough details to differentiate it from others in the same class.

EXAMPLES

Possibly the most common pattern of development, examples provide constant support for assertions as the paper unfolds.

ANALOGY

To draw comparisons between items that appear to have little in common. This writing form is developed for various reasons: to provide clarity to something considered abstract; to argue a point; to make the unknown known; and to provide new insight on a previously understood position.

CAUSE AND EFFECT

The effect is often established in the paragraph and then followed by a list of causes. Or, the paragraph may establish causes and then develop the body around the effects.

PROCESS ANALYSIS

This form is usually chronological and based on a time sequence. The point of process analysis is to show readers how to perform a process or to actually describe how a process is performed.

CLASSIFICATION/DIVISION

To group items, based on a consistent principle, into categories. Division follows the same definition, differing only in the fact that it merely divides an item into parts.

literature vs social commentary

Many student writers often say, "I feel like I keep retelling the published literature." This uncertainty makes students feel like they are not developing original thought, and, instead, they wonder if they are merely repeating what a published work has already established. To avoid this, the CHART or Scaffolding Format must be specific to the point YOU are trying to make. Remember, the approach to the literary work is only a platform—a reading that has INSPIRED you to write, using the initial text as the example to prove the point you want to make on the topic that grabbed your intention. As such, the body paragraphs must provide a balance between an examination of the literature and social commentary. One without the other loses the context: too much literature is like a prong specific book report; too much social commentary loses the literature and talks around it—not through it.

Example:

In Naomi Wolf's controversial "The Making of a Slut," she establishes that, in both grammar school and high school, her voluptuous friend Dinah was the victim of social backlash because of her socio-economic status. The author points out that the resentment the talented dancer experienced was a direct result of being "poorer than the other white kids" (Wolf 56). Throughout history, girls developing into womanhood have battled gender prejudice. In urban areas like Brooklyn, girls reaching sexual maturity–a physical, chemical, and mental change that begins during early teen development–have often been bullied because they are seen as poor and vulnerable. Moreover, as they become women, "females are often subjected to resentment that is intentionally targeted at what is perceived as a social weakness" (Jones 6). Nothing, according to "The Hatred from My Sisters," addresses this painful pubescent development like the reality that "no one hates the female species, like females" (Barnes para. 4). This is exactly the point Wolf is trying to make. Her argument is hammered home when she says, "There was no visual language in our world for a poor girl with big breasts walking tall except 'slut'" (55). Of course, the question surrounding the attack on girls like Dinah is simple: why?

editing your essay

PAPER GUIDELINES

Once your draft is finished, fine tune your writing by paying attention to issues relating to content, structure, language, and mechanics. Initially, use the following editing guidelines by yourself. For best results, always solicit a respected peer to read over your work.

Look at this example of a typical English department guideline for developing an **A** paper:

Content: The paper shows a grasp of the full assignment. It clearly states and explores a complex argument or thesis with thoughtful, specific analysis. The paper is written with coherence and clarity; it develops connections among texts or the student's own ideas, and summarizes events, ideas, or sources only to advance the argument, not provide filler.

Structure: The paper's structure reflects logical thinking. Paragraphs are well developed with precise use of detail and appropriate transitions. Quotations are selected to advance the argument and support the thesis, not to provide filler; they are introduced smoothly, enclosed in quotation marks, and properly cited. The paper adheres to the assignment's length requirements.

Sophistication of Language: The paper shows excellent control of language, appropriate use of vocabulary, and varied sentence structure.

Mechanics: Errors, if any, are typological rather than an indication of problems with grammar; the paper is virtually error-free. The paper is in the required format, follows the proper system of documentation, and is handed in on time.

Below is the guideline for a paper that has not been thoroughly proofread or edited, resulting in a **C** grade:

Content: The thesis of the paper is an acceptable response to the basic argument, but is presented in too general and vague a manner, and more detail and clarity are needed. The paper relies mostly on brief assertions or a summary of texts without much explanation or commentary, but the assertions make sense or the summaries are essentially clear and accurate. Connections among texts are stated, but not discussed in much detail.

Structure: The supporting ideas are related to the thesis but are not presented in a logical order or developed with adequate specifics. Lack of transitions and other disjunctions force the reader to infer what the writer means. Paragraphs set up ideas but are not developed adequately. Quotations are dropped into the text without introduction or discussion, are often not the best evidence for the points they are used to support, and are too long. The paper meets the length requirements, but the writer is self-evident rather than thoughtful or perceptive.

Sophistication of Language: Sentences and phrases express the thesis and supporting ideas but are repetitive in pattern. Occasional run-ons and fragments show problems with sentence boundaries. Vocabulary is usually appropriate to the subject matter, but not precise enough to express complex thoughts.

Mechanics: The paper follows format and documentation requirements overall, but shows grammatical or sentence-level errors or patterns of error.

Developed by NYCCT's English Department, City University of New York

Review checklist:

Check the **flow** of the ideas. Do you like their overall arrangement? Does the paper follow a standard writing pattern (chronological/emphatic/simple to complex/spatial)? Does it make good use of standard writing forms (description/comparison and contrast/cause and effect)?

Is your **thesis** made clear in a three-pronged thesis statement? Is your thesis reflected in your title?

Vocabulary: Did you use a thesaurus to be as precise and appropriately sophisticated as possible?

Repetitiousness: Unnecessary repetition of the same words, phrases, and/or sentence types.

Redundancy is repetition of the same idea in different words.

"In this modern world of today in which we live," for example, says nothing more than "today," but says it four different ways.

Vague Spots: This is an area in your writing development that makes a reader wonder what, exactly, is being said or asserted.

Transitions allow for a smooth **flow** that connects sentences and paragraphs. Make sure the paper reads as one fluid piece of writing instead of different paragraphs lacking connection and cohesion.

A Conclusion that leads to a revealing point and is not repetitive or redundant.

PEER REVIEW

Always have someone whose insight and skill you respect look at the document. Ask them to respond to each of these questions:

Does the **title** accurately and imaginatively capture the gist of the essay?

Does the **introduction** capture your attention? Does it fully introduce the paper's topic and focus? Does it contain a working thesis?

Are the body paragraphs focused? Do they start with effective **topic sentences**?

Are **transitions** sufficient and appropriate, ensuring smooth reading? Does the last sentence of each paragraph prepare the reader for the following paragraph?

Are there any **awkward sentences** that are difficult to understand? Are the verb tenses consistent and appropriate?

Are there **words** missing within a sentence? Are any of the words used incorrectly? Can you suggest better ones?

Are there any **misspelled** words?

Is **punctuation** used correctly?

Are **quotes** used correctly and effectively? Do they begin with appropriate **signal phrases**? Are authors and page numbers cited correctly?

Is the **conclusion** compelling, and does it lead to an overall point for the reader?

Sometimes, an instructor may ask you to work with a classmate. When this happens, use the following checklist:

Classroom Peer Review

1. Use symbols (stars, underlines, squiggly lines), special notations, or commonly used proofreading symbols (see next box) to indicate strengths, awkward sentences, confusing parts, breaks in logic, misspelled words, poor punctuation, or lack of descriptive development.
2. Discuss what you really like about your peer's essay.
3. Consider whether or not you would still understand what was written if you removed the discussion of the literature from the essay.
4. Locate your peer's thesis.
5. Consider whether or not the thesis and the essay satisfy the requirements for the assignment.
6. Do the body paragraphs in your peer's essay back up his/her thesis?
7. List 5 things your peer can do to improve the essay.

Developed by Robert Ostrom, NYCCT, CUNY

PROOFREADING

Before handing in your essay, **proofread** and look for oversights. For example, make sure you have a title that reflects your paper's content, typos, and formatting errors.

Commonly Used Proofreading Symbols

A. LANGUAGE AND STYLE

1. ww = wrong word
2. om = omit
3. rep = repetition of same or similar words
4. awk = awkward
5. WC = word choice

B. CONTENT AND ORGANIZATION

1. ¶ = new paragraph needed
2. dev = more development needed
3. red = redundant (repetition of same or similar ideas)
4. trans = transition needed
5. QCSA = Quotes cannot stand alone.

C. SYNTAX

1. r-o = run-on sentence
2. frag = sentence fragment
3. mm = misplaced modifier
4. // = faulty parallelism

D. GRAMMAR

1. ag = agreement error
2. vp = vague pronoun
3. vt = verb tense error

E. PROOFREADING DETAILS

1. cap = capitalization
2. sp = spelling
3. / = spacing needed
4. > = indent

1 2 3 4 **5**

Writing the Research Essay

At almost every stage of your academic career, the research paper will be an inevitable requirement. As such, the ability to develop an argument based on a specific topic in an organized manner is a skill that should be learned BEFORE you take advanced classes. In these higher level courses, instructors generally WILL NOT teach paper structure and style. Instead, they will ask you to establish and defend an argument based on some aspect of the course lessons using secondary sources. They WILL NOT teach you how to compose the essay because those skills should have been learned in a class dedicated to writing development. Whether you have been asked to write a three page paper or a sixty page graduate thesis, all essay writing does the same thing, regardless of length and complexity: introduce, defend, and conclude.

Even though research writing is based upon a primary source(s)—a central novel, poem, article, concept, film, empirical study, or field of discussion—along with secondary source(s)—writing that supports ideas and concepts that YOUR thesis and paragraph assertions establish—the voice of the paper must be YOURS. Keep in mind that whether assigned a broad topic or a specific focus, you will be expected to establish a position, defend it, and conclude while incorporating source materials throughout.

If assigned a broad topic, particularly one where you have no strong opinion or knowledge, research can provide clarity and give you an understanding that now allows for an argument to develop. As you begin to write and develop your own voice on the matter discussed, the secondary sources can now be used to balance out your argument and allow your reader to understand just how developed and investigated the paper is.

Research can be overwhelming. If not focused, you may begin a process that makes the challenge of writing more frustrating. To avoid this, refer to THE CHART on page 76. Once your paper becomes more concise, you'll find that the elements that should be researched are already outlined.

the abstract

You may be asked to submit an abstract for a proposed or completed work. The abstract, a formal document, provides a short, insightful description of a larger researched document. Instructors will often require that an abstract be submitted and approved before the larger work is done, or that it is introduced separately in the opening of the final submitted document. Depending on the reason for the abstract— research proposal, research project, experiment, thesis, dissertation, review, conference submission, grant writing, call for papers—the abstract is usually a 100-250 word description of what the larger document will reveal. The proposed work is often written in the first person, the "I will..." voice, while the completed work is generally written in the "This essay, behavior, or research examines..." voice. Both approaches generally break down into four succinct categories that speak to the totality of the larger paper: **what** the paper is going to do—its purpose; **why** the paper is relevant and what it intends to establish; **how**—the paper's methodology, the research process or writing technique you will utilize to prove your argument; and a **conclusion**, which is the final result, and the implication of the result on the intended audience. It should be accurate, brief, and clear.

Note: The abstract is **NOT** a summary or a critique of the larger document.

secondary sources

The only purpose for using a secondary source(s) in your writing is to support the argument your thesis, or the assertions within your developing sentences, are making. Secondary sources should not overwhelm the writer's voice. They should only be used to support the writer and add validity to some statement being established in the paper. If the secondary sources become the primary voice in the paper, there has been an abuse of researched materials. When this is done, the paper does not showcase the writer's ability to develop a critical voice that speaks to a specified audience.

HOW TO EVALUATE SOURCE MATERIAL

Consider the following as you select primary and secondary sources to support your research:

1. Is the material dated?

2. Does the author have a bias?

Note: This does not mean the source is not valid or credible, but addressing the bias in your writing removes any uncertainty about your scholarship.

3. The impact of technology.

Note: Has the argument changed because of advancments in technology, e.g. Social Media?

4. How well-written is the source? Are there typos, misspelled words, inaccuracies?

finding sources

Finding appropriate, up-to-date sources is crucial for the success of your research essay. If you wish to work from primary sources, you may need to go outside the classroom to investigate the holdings at a museum, to interview experts, or perhaps to examine the architecture of a particular neighborhood. Often, however, the library is your best single source of information. Its holdings include books, encyclopedias, journals, magazines, and newspapers that you may find useful. Thanks to remarkable innovations in technology, the library is also where you can go to access powerful research databases. Nowadays, these databases are often accessible via your own computer, once you have set up your account using your college ID. As long as you have a current college ID, students at a linked University system like City University of New York (CUNY), City Colleges of Chicago (CCC), The University of California (UC system) are allowed to borrow books from any of their sister colleges.

Your librarian will show you how to find the many databases that can lead you to a book, an article, or even primary source material. Two databases particularly helpful for accessing newspaper and journal articles are **Academic Search Premier (EBSCO)** and **LexisNexis**. Although available online, these databases are not websites. They are collections of articles that have been reformatted and placed within a database.

To get to these databases, go to your library's website. Under "Research Tools," click on "Databases A–Z." You will find a wide array of databases arranged alphabetically. **Academic Search Premier (EBSCO)** appears first.

Using these databases demands that you use key words. For example, in an essay on the effects of global warming on disease patterns, you might type in "global warming," "diseases," and "increase" as key words.

Find: global warming

[AND] diseases

[AND] increase

Helpful Hints

1. **Be sure to click on the "full text" box,** which will ensure that you get the complete article rather than just a summary and bibliographic information.

2. **Indicate the timeframe of your article.** You can choose a range by month and year (or simply leave blank if you don't want to limit your search in this way). The most recently published article will appear first. Keep in mind that a dated article may not have the same relevance as a more current one.

3. **Click on the appropriate box if you want a scholarly or peer-reviewed article.** A refereed journal article means that is has been carefully scrutinized by other professionals in the field for quality and accuracy.

4. **Indicate the publication type:** periodical, newspaper, book, or "all."

5. If you get too many entries, **limit your search** further. If you don't get enough entries, try new key words or check your spelling.

6. You will find that your articles will appear by title. Sometimes you can determine if an article is right for you just by this. If not, **click on the title and you will link to an abstract**, or summary, of the article as well as bibliographic information.

7. You may also wish to **skim your article**, paying extra close attention to the introduction and conclusion to determine its relevance to your topic.

8. Once you find an article that looks like it might be worth reading more closely, directly **email it to your own email account.** Don't forget to give this email a helpful subject header so you'll recall what this email is all about at a later time.

9. For each source you plan on using, **be sure that you have all necessary bibliographic information**. You will need this information for your "in-text" citations and to create your Bibliography/Works Cited/References page. Be sure you have the name of the author/ editor, the title of the article or book, the title of the magazine, newspaper, or host website (if applicable), the date of publication, relevant page numbers, and, for books, publication information (city, publishing company, and date). For Internet sources, you will also need the date you visited the site and the URL (address of the site) or other information needed to access the site.

FYI

Below is a list of great Links to use for credible and specific sources:

Ebsco	Medline Plus
JSTOR	NBER
Google Scholar	DOAJ
Microsoft Academic Search	U.S. Census Bureau
Google Books	

Note: Broad Web search engines—Yahoo, Google, Bing—are not designed to bring the best academic results. They are perfect for shopping, reading reviews, searching for hotels or flights. As such, they may make the research process overwhelming. Below are eleven sites and their descriptions that are either discipline specific or easy to navigate.

Research Resources	
PubMed	Database of medical literature.
CIA World Factbook	Statistics, reports, maps, history, and other information on 267 countries.
JURN	Search engine for humanities research.
National Crime Justice Reference Services	Database of articles about issues pertaining to various aspects of the justice system.
OAIster	Feature-rich search tool for a variety of different sources.
Bureau of Economic Research	Database of economic papers.
Refseek	General-purpose search engine that finds books, websites, academic papers, and newspapers.
Sweet Search	A search engine especially for students. Every site has been selected by research experts.

PhilPapers	A database for academic papers related to philosophy.
IPl2	Search engine and an index of credible sites arranged by topic.
Directory of Open Access Journals	A database of scholarly scientific information.

incorporating material

Ultimately, the point of your research is to gather ideas to develop and support your thesis. **Summarizing, paraphrasing**, and **quoting** are the three ways to bring information found in your readings into your own work. Because the ideas drawn from your sources are not original to you, you will have to credit your author and source. This is called a citation. An in-text citation is when you identify your author and source in your essay. An "end" citation appears in your Bibliography/Works Cited/References page. Crediting your sources prevents accusations of plagiarism and allows your own reader to investigate a particular topic or idea further.

SUMMARIZING

A summary is when you condense a substantial amount of material into a paragraph or perhaps a single sentence. You can summarize the main idea of a long passage, an article, or even a whole book. Summaries are used when you don't want to provide too many details, just a central idea.

Here is an example of a summary of a passage from Susan Strasser's book *Waste and Want*:

Original Source:

Most Americans produced little trash before the twentieth century. Packaged goods were becoming popular as the century began, but merchants continued to sell most food, hardware, and cleaning products in bulk. Their customers practiced habits of reuse that had prevailed in agricultural communities here and abroad. Women boiled food scraps into soup or fed them to domestic animals; chickens, especially, would eat almost anything and returned the favor with eggs. Durable items were passed on to people of other classes or generations, or stored in attics or basements for later use. Objects of no use to adults became playthings for children (12).

Summary: Up until the last century, Americans were superb recyclers and reusers, who rarely threw out much of anything (Strasser 12).

THE ANNOTATED BIBLIOGRAPHY

When it comes time to write your research essay, your professor might even ask for an **Annotated Bibliography**. This simply means that for every source you use, you will need to briefly summarize it.

Example of an annotated citation:

Strasser, Susan. *Waste and Want: A Social History of Trash.* New York: Metropolitan Books, 1999. Print.

Waste and Want: A Social History of Trash examines how over the last hundred years, advertisers have caused Americans to massively increase their consumer habits leading to waste on a previously unimaginable scale.

PARAPHRASING

A paraphrase is like a summary in that you put the ideas of others into your own words. Whereas a summary reports what a source says in significantly fewer words than the source, a paraphrase retells the information of a source in approximately the same number of words, clinging much more closely to the intent and content of a particular line or passage. Be careful not to follow your source's wording too closely as this will constitute plagiarism.

Here is an example of a paraphrase of the same passage by Strasser.

Paraphrase:
Unlike consumer practices today, Americans before the twentieth century rarely threw anything out. Instead, they either recycled or reused products such as metals, food scraps, and other goods. Also preventing waste was the fact that most merchants did not package the products they sold (Strasser 12).

QUOTING

Incorporating the voices of others can usefully be used to make your own argument stronger. However, you need to take care whether to paraphrase or quote directly.

When to quote:

—the language of the speaker is particularly vivid

—you need to maintain technical accuracy

—the exact words of a speaker are important

—the speaker holds important authority

—when you are discussing the language itself, as in poetry or literature.

A quote consists of the exact words from a source, as the following example illustrates:

As late as 1882, reports Susan Strasser in Waste and Want: A Social History of Trash, *a manual on teaching children household economy had to define a wastebasket for readers: "It is for collecting all the torn and useless pieces of paper, and should be emptied every day, care being taken that nothing of value is thus thrown away" (12).*

As the above example shows, it is good style to lead into quotations gracefully and fluidly. This is generally accomplished by using signal phrases. A signal phrase is exactly that: a phrase that signals that a quote is coming. Here is a list of useful signal phrases:

According to Susan Strasser, *"Most Americans produced little trash before the twentieth century" (12).*

As Susan Strasser writes, *"Most Americans produced little trash before the twentieth century" (12).*

Susan Strasser points out that *"Most Americans produced little trash before the twentieth century" (12).*

"Most Americans produced little trash before the twentieth century" (12), **as Susan Strasser claims.**

In the words of Susan Strasser, *". . ."*

Some other verbs used in signal phrases:

acknowledges, adds, admits, argues, asserts, believes, comments, contends, insists, notes, observes, reasons, rejects, suggests, posits

Note: Generally speaking, signal phrases are written in the present tense.

Setting off long quotes:

When the quote you want to use is more than four typed lines of prose, you must indent the entire quote one inch from the left margin. Be sure also to double-space the long quote. You also need to drop the quotation marks as the indention by itself signals that the passage is a direct quote. Note also how the end punctuation of the quoted material now precedes the parenthetical citation.

For example:

Susan Strasser gives many examples of how earlier Americans understood the importance of saving and reusing:

> *Most Americans produced little trash before the twentieth century. Packaged goods were becoming popular as the century began, but merchants continued to sell most food, hardware, and cleaning products in bulk. Their customers practiced habits of reuse that had prevailed in agricultural communities here and abroad. Women boiled food scraps into soup or fed them to domestic animals; chickens, especially, would eat almost anything and returned the favor with eggs. Durable items were passed on to people of other classes or generations, or stored in attics or basements for later use. Objects of no use to adults became playthings for children. (12)*

defining and avoiding plagiarism

In writing, plagiarism is defined as an act or instance of imitating the language and thoughts of an author without authorization, as well as the representation of that author's work as one's own. It means to steal or pass off ideas or words from another as one's own—to literally commit literary theft.

Thanks to technology, plagiarism now extends to copying media, making a video using copyrighted music or footage, performing copyrighted material, copying a different medium, altering copyrighted images or audio, even if done in an original way.

Using Signal phrases, introducing authors fully, and citing paraphrased works will help eliminate plagiarism. The advent of the Internet has made the temptation to plagiarize more tempting than ever. Please understand that it is not a small violation of writing rules. It is a crime.

Note: If unsure, cite. The worst that can happen is that someone says the citation is unnecessary. Contrastingly, being accused of plagiarism is a crime that can cost you your standing in a class (failing class), your academic integrity (suspension or expulsion), or result in a legal lawsuit.

WHY CITE?

Keep in mind that you are doing three things when citing sources:

- Giving credit to other writers for their ideas
- Showing your audience where to find the sources used in your research
- Protecting yourself from being accused of academic and/or publishing dishonesty

COMMON KNOWLEDGE AND PARAPHRASING

Common knowledge can be described as facts known by most educated people. To say that the Japanese attacked Pearl Harbor on December 7, 1941 is an example of common knowledge and need not be cited. What is not common knowledge must be documented. When taking notes, put "quotations" around sentences and phrases that you take directly from the text, and be sure to record the source. Is your statement paraphrased? That is, are you expressing someone else's ideas in your own words? If so, it too must be documented. A good paraphrase uses your own voice; a bad one borrows too heavily from the original.

	EXAMPLE	PLAGIARISM? YES OR NO
Original text from John Keegan's *The Battle for History*	The history of the Second World War has not yet been written . . . the passions it aroused still run too high, the wounds it inflicted still cut too deep, and the unresolved problems it left still bulk too large . . . to strike an objective balance.[1]	
Acceptable quotation from original text	Military historian Sir John Keegan argues that "The history of the Second World War has not yet been written . . . [because] the passions it aroused still run too high, the wounds it inflicted still cut too deep, and the unresolved problems it left still bulk too large . . . to strike an objective balance" (30).	No
Acceptable paraphrase	Military historian Sir John Keegan maintains that no one has written the true history of the Second World War yet because the conflict was so complicated, aroused such passion, and left too many issues unsettled for anyone today to write a balanced account of it (30).	No

Unacceptable paraphrase	The true history of the Second World War hasn't been written yet because the struggle was so complicated, the passions the war aroused still too high, and the wounds still too deep for historians to write an objective account.	Yes
Acceptable. Student's original thought in his own voice.	The history of World War Two is very complex, too complex for an accurate understanding at this present time.	No

[1]Keegan, John. *The Battle for History: Re-fighting World War II*

documenting your sources

Whenever you use information, ideas, or words derived from someone else's work, you must give credit to that person using what is known as a **citation**. The exception to this rule is when you use information that is common knowledge, such as birthdates, the chemical composition of water, or the names of the planets. How sources are documented or cited varies by field and discipline, and you should use the style appropriate to your field. However, whether you follow the MLA style—appropriate for research in the humanities—or the APA style—designed for the Social Sciences—the basic aims and rules of documentation are similar. To reiterate, **whenever using the ideas from another author and source, you must let your reader know who and where your information comes from**.

When to cite your source

- A direct quotation
- Information that you have paraphrased or summarized
- A statistic
- Someone else's idea or opinion
- Concrete facts
- Illustrations and graphs (not your own)
- Information not commonly known

Your identification of an author and source should appear immediately after you present information in what is known as an **in-text (parenthetical) citation**. A detailed list of your sources will also appear at the end of your paper on a separate Bibliography, Works Cited, or Reference page.

Note: No matter what the style manual calls it, they are all bibliography pages.

Note: Sometimes footnotes or endnotes are used are used to provide additional information about a topic that is not essential to the main point of your essay.

MLA DOCUMENTATION

If your instructor asks you to use the MLA (Modern Language Association) style of documentation, it is for a specific reason. Normally, disciplines within the liberal arts and the humanities require this style of writing. MLA documentation requires that the writer document his/her sources using a specific set of guidelines. These guidelines are specific to a myriad of details. However, the main areas of concern for most student writers are the use of font size, spacing, pagination, margins, quotes and subsequent in-text citations, and the sources listed on the bibliography, otherwise known as the Works Cited page in the MLA style of writing.

MLA FONT: Size 12 font

MLA MARGINS: 1 inch all around

SPACING: The entire document must be double spaced. The first line of each new paragraph must be indented. There should be one space between each new sentence.

PAGINATION: Use Arabic numerals only (1, 2, 3, 4)

MLA in-text citations

Citations are required for all print and electronic sources. These are examples of the most common.

Author's name in the main sentence

When you identify the author in the main sentence, provide only the page number in your parentheses.

Lillian Hammer asserts that all fiction comes from a real place; as such, fiction is somewhat autobiographical (342).

Note: In the main sentence, provide the full name when you first indicate the author and last name only if you use the name again.

Author's name and page number in parentheses

When you do not identify the author in the main sentence, provide both the author's last name and page number in parentheses.

All fiction comes from a real place; as such, fiction is somewhat autobiographical (Hammer 342).

More than one author

When a source has two or three authors, include their last names and page number. (If a source has four or more authors, include only the first author's name followed by "et al.")

Henry Louis Gates is easily one of America's greatest authors, but his place within the literary cannon and his impact on and representations of the African American community have been hotly debated over the last two decades (Cornelius and Mac 56).

Unknown author

When the author of an article is not given or unknown, include the title of the source instead as well as the page number.

An anonymous review of Walt Whitman, appearing in 1855, accused the author of "cultivating sinister thoughts in the minds of young men and women" ("A Poem Bent on Destruction" 31).

No page number (often in the case of online articles)

When a page number of your source is not provided, simply provide the author's last name. If a Web source numbers its paragraphs or screens, provide the paragraph number indicating this with the abbreviation *par(s)*.

Even after Whitman was condemned as a raving lunatic by the public at large, his relationship to his mother remained close (Reynolds par. 13).

More than one source

To cite more than one source, give the citations in alphabetical order and separate them with a semicolon.

Several scholars have argued that the modern urban poem was invented by Walt Whitman and later perfected by Frank O'Hara (Pryor 58; Williams 67).

Organization as author

If the author is an organization, provide this information instead.

Whitman's work was at first influenced by the Ralph Waldo Emerson, but he came into his own upon the publication of "Song of Myself" (The Whitman Society 35).

Secondhand quotations

When you quote an actual quote within your source, use "qtd. in" (quoted in).

Annette Saddik, author of many fine books on playwright Tennessee Williams, refers to the years between 1960 and 1966 as the "saddest period of his life yet also his most experimental" (qtd. in Guida 151).

In this example, though the quote is from Annette Saddik, it appears in a work by Guida. In your Works Cited page, Guida, not Saddik will be listed.

MLA Works Cited Page

In addition to providing **in-text citations**, you also need to list your sources and relevant bibliographic information in a separate **Works Cited page**. This page has a very specific format. For example, it must be organized alphabetically by your author's last name, indented properly (all lines after the first), and double-spaced (owing to space considerations, examples are shown single-spaced). The bibliographic information that you need to provide varies somewhat from source to source but generally includes the author's full name, the title of the piece, the date of publication, and the publisher.

MLA now requires that you indicate the format of the source used: Web, this includes date viewed, Print, DVD, and so forth.

The following are sample entries for the most commonly used types of sources. If you have a source not covered here, consult MLA.org or an MLA website such as the comprehensive one found at Purdue OWL (owl.english.purdue.edu).

Books

Book by a Single Author: Author, *Title*. City: Publisher, date, and medium of publication.

Barlow, Aaron. *Star Power: The Impact of Branded Celebrity*. Santa Barbara: Praeger, 2014. Print.

Note: Only the first line is at the margin; all other lines are indented five spaces.

Book by Two or More Authors: Authors, *Title*. City: Publisher, date, and medium of publication.

Ferrell, Monique and Julian Williams. *Good Writing Made Simple*. Dubuque: Kendall Hunt, 2015. Print.

Note: Only the first author's name is inverted; the remaining name(s) are in regular order.

Anthology by a Single Editor: Editor, *Title*. City: Publisher, date.

Durgin, Allen, ed. *Readings on American Literature, Culture, and Art.* New York: Norton, 2008. Print.

Anthology by Two or More Editors: Editors, *Title*. City: Publisher, date, and medium of publication.

Ferrell, Monique and Julian Williams, eds. *Lead, Follow, or Move Out of the Way: Global Perspectives in Literature and Film.* Dubuque: Kendall Hunt, 2015. Print.

Note: Only the first editor's name is inverted.

Article or Story in an Anthology or a Chapter in an Edited Book

Ali, Mohammed Naseehu. "Mallam Sile." *Lead, Follow, or Move Out of The Way: Global Perspectives Literature and Film.* Eds. Monique Ferrell and Julian Williams. Dubuque: Kendall Hunt, 2012. 286-294. Print.

Note: Since articles are only a part of a larger work, you must also provide your reader with page numbers. The numbers should be for the whole article, not just for the pages you have used.

Articles in Newspapers and Periodicals

Newspaper Article: Author, "Title" (of article), *Title* (of newspaper), date: page numbers (and section if any).

Fullerton, Jennifer. "Congestion Pricing: A Bad Idea Whose Time Has Not Come." *New York Times* 12 Oct. 2006: A7–8. Print.

Note: Recall that the titles of short pieces such as articles are in quotation marks and the titles of long pieces such as newspaper are underlined or italicized.

Article from a Magazine: Author, "Title" (of article), *Title* (of magazine), date: page numbers.

Frazier, Ian. "Take the F." *New Yorker* Nov. 2006: 24–34. Print.

Article in a Scholarly Journal: Author, "Title" (of article), *Title* (of journal), volume number/issue number (date): page numbers.

Peters, Debrise. "The Doubt." *Latin American Quarterly* 14.3 (2014): 16-27. Print.

Unsigned Article:

If no author is given for an article, begin with the title and alphabetize the title.

"Fighting Crime in America." *Time* 6 Apr. 2007: 37–45. Print.

Online Sources

Citing online articles is different from citing articles from printed newspapers and magazines in that you need to identify not only the publication date of the article but the date you accessed it. Providing the Web address (URL) is only required if necessary to find the source, and then as briefly as possible. If you can Google the title, you don't need the URL. Titles should be underlined or placed in italics. In recent years, the use of italics has become more common, but either is acceptable. Just remember to be consistent.

Article from an Online Periodical: Author. "Title" (of Article). *Title* (of periodical). Publication date. Web. Access date (date you accessed it).

Loss, Rau. "Eating The Blues." *Salon*. 9 April 2013. Web. 6 May 2014.

Article found on a Library Database: Author. "Title" (of Article). *Title* (of periodical). Publication date. Name of Database. Location of Library Database. Web. Access date.

Posnock, Ross. "Singing the Blues During the Great Depression." *Salon*. 18 April 2002. *EBSCO-Academic Premier*. New York City College of Technology. Web. 3 May 2006.

Institutional Website: Title of Website (underline). Sponsoring Institution (if any). Web. Access Date.

Making of America. Cornell University. Web. 30 Oct. 2007.

Personal Website: Person responsible for site. Title of site (underline). Name of associated institution or organization (if any). Web. Date of access.

Glows, Kelly. *The World of Better Thinkers*. University of Colorado. Web. 3 May 2013.

Blog or Discussion Group: Name of author. "Title [or subject line of posting]." Blog [or Online posting]. Web. Date of posting. Date viewed.

Louie, Auguste. "Dining In the Big Easy." Blog. 14 Feb. 2014. Web. 25 Sept. 2014.

Film

Title (underlined). Director. Format. Distributor. Year Produced. If relevant, list performers.

Gangs of New York. Dir. Martin Scorcese. DVD. Paramount Pictures, 1996.

Imitation of Life. Dir. Douglas Sirk. Perf. Lana Turner, Juanita Moore, John Gavin, Sandra Dee. DVD. Universal International Pictures, 1959.

Interview

Name. Position. Personal Interview. Location. Date.

Falvey, Kate [Owner, Creative Books]. Personal Interview. Brooklyn, NY. 2
June 2008.

Sample Works Cited Page in MLA Style

Works Cited

[Note: sources without authors appear first]

"Fighting Crime in America." *Time* 6 Apr. 2007: 37–45. Print.

Making of America. Cornell University. Web. 30 Oct. 2007.

Barlow, Aaron. *Blogging America: From Benjamin Franklin to Today's Citizen
Journalists.* New York: Praeger, 2007. Print.

Falvey, Kate [Owner, Creative Books]. Personal Interview. Brooklyn, NY.
2 June 2008.

Gold, Shoshana. "Eating in Brooklyn." Blog. 21 June 2008. Web. 25 June
2008.

Frazier, Ian. "Take the F." *New Yorker* Nov. 2006: 24–34. Print.

Fullerton, Jennifer. "Congestion Pricing: A Bad Idea Whose Time Has
Not Come." *New York Times* 12 Oct. 2006: A7–8. Print.

Posnock, Ross. "Rock and Roll in the 1950s" *Salon.* 20 June 2005. Web.
3 May 2006.

-----. "Singing the Blues During the Great Depression." *Salon.* 18
April 2002. *EBSCO-Academic Premier.* New York City College of
Technology. Web. 3 May 2006.

[Note: use five hyphens if you list an author more than once]

Sands, Jeremiah. "The Whiteness of Melville's Whale." *American Quarterly*
13.3 (2005): 77–85. Print.

Whitehead, Colson. "The Colossus of New York." *The Place Where We
Dwell: Reading and Writing About New York City.* Eds. Juanita But and
Mark Noonan. Dubuque: Kendall Hunt, 2007. 50–76. Print.

Sample Research Paper in MLA Style

Your Name
Instructor's name
Course
Date
Type of Assignment

Solar Power:

A Catalyst for a Sustainable Future

Title is centered.

It is an undeniable truth that every minute aspect of life, in one way or another, depends on the sun for energy. Solar power is a renewable energy source that is derived directly from the sun through both heat and sunlight. Though not a new phenomenon, demand for it has recently escalated all over the world. Some may be familiar with this type of energy as it is used to power household products such as calculators, flashlights, and certain toys. However, on a much larger scale, solar energy is also used to power houses, corporate buildings, and even large cities. Unfortunately, most cities have not converted to solar energy use and still rely on fossil fuels such as coal, oil, and natural gases that are, of course, nonrenewable and becoming less abundant. Unlike these fossil fuels, solar power does not release carbon dioxide, sulfur dioxide, nitrogen oxide, or mercury into the atmosphere. It is a completely clean and natural way to generate energy without the need to burn fuel and generate emission. Aside from halting the emissions that cause global warming, solar energy is virtually maintenance free. And for those who reside in the U.S., the government offers a tax credit of up to $2,000 for solar panel users (Bocchine 2). Solar power is clearly the answer to saving our planet, while saving money over the long run.

Opening sentences capture readers' attention.

Author's last name is given in parentheses. Since website article does not have page numbers, the author refers to the page number of the version she printed out (paragraph numbers can also be used when no page numbers are given).

Thesis asserts student's main point.

----There are now two main processes of obtaining solar power. The first is a thermal process that involves mounting a parabola-shaped mirror panel that focuses light onto a black pipe with a heat-transfer fluid inside. The fluid is used to boil water into steam, which, in turn, rotates a turbine that produces electricity [see Fig. 1]. The latter, which most people are familiar with, requires the installation of photovoltaic panels, made of silicon that then convert sunlight directly into electricity [see Fig. 2]. This process is typically more expensive than solar

thermal power and requires intense light to function at its ideal capacity. Another problem is that to generate energy on a large scale, hundreds of panels must be placed in open areas such as

deserts, often endangering the habitats of animals such as the desert tortoise. Accordingly, environmentalists in California are taking steps to reduce the use of photovoltaic panels and increase solar thermal power use. This is now possible, for, as Donald E. Brandt, Chief Executive of Pinnacle West, explains, "solar

thermal power has advanced . . . beyond the demonstration stage" (qtd. in Wald 2).

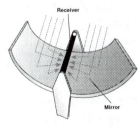

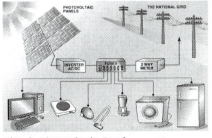

Fig. 1. Parabola-Shaped Mirror Panel.

Fig. 2. Photovoltaic Panel.

Despite challenges, solar power is creating new means of environmentally efficient energy in cities all around the world. In the U.S., California, Nevada, and Arizona have already begun making strides towards creating these solar cities. In June 2006, the U.S. Conference of Mayors adopted the "2030 Challenge" with goals of reducing the greenhouse gas emissions from all future city building by 50 percent by the year 2030. This will also ensure that all new buildings are carbon neutral (Beatley 31). Recently, in New York City, Mayor Michael R. Bloomberg has taken the initiative to update the city's current solar electric capacity by proposing that the City Department of Administrative Services (DCAS) allow private solar developers to purchase, install, own, and maintain solar panels on city-owned buildings in all five boroughs (Brown 2). This plan, which is part of *PlaNYC*, would allow for two megawatts of electricity in such areas. According to Matthew Wald, one megawatt is enough energy to run 1,000 room air-conditioners at once (1). With Bloomberg's plan, the dependence on carbon-based fuels will be greatly reduced. As the Mayor rightly boasts,

> New York City is moving ahead vigorously
> on our *PlaNYC* agenda, especially in
> the all-important area of reducing our
> reliance on the carbon-based fuels that
> contribute to global warming. We've
> set a target of shrinking our carbon
> footprint by 30% by the year 2030.
> Increasing the use of renewable energy,
> like solar power, is a key strategy in
> that effort. Using solar power decreases
> demand for electricity from the power
> grid, which is typically generated by
> burning the fossil fuels that contribute
> to climate change. (qtd. in Brown 1)

Author's name is given in parentheses; page number refers to print journal.

Since author is introduced in signal phrase, only the page number is needed.

Long quotation is indented ten spaces; quotation marks are omitted; end punctuation appears before citation.

Impressively, in shrinking our carbon footprint by 30 percent by the year 2030, a 10 million metric ton reduction of emission per year can be expected.

> The author makes good use of transition sentence here.

This proposal would not only boost the environment but the economy as well. Under Bloomberg's proposal, the New York City Solar America Initiative (SAI)—a partnership between CUNY, New York City Economic Development Corporation (NYCEDC), and the Mayor's Office of Long-term Planning and Sustainability—will promote a U.S. based solar industry which will create 30,000 new jobs in the field. It has been hard in the past to fund such projects, but the Solar Initiative has been gaining more and more followers as its feasibility and necessity grow increasingly more distinct.

> Article cited has two authors.

According to the Energy Department, solar power currently constitutes for about 2 or 3 percent of the electricity in the U.S. (Revkin and Wald 2). More and more, however, cities around the globe are looking to the sky for the most powerful yet underrated source of energy. Barcelona, Perth, and Freiburg, for example, have committed themselves to underwriting solar development on a massive scale (Beatley 34). Freiburg, in particular, has "adopted an impressive and wide-ranging set of environmental planning and sustainability initiatives" and has come to be known as the "ecological capital of Europe" (Beatley 35). The U.S. also needs to follow the lead of Sweden, which is extremely progressive in its reliance on renewable energy and clean energy vehicles. In Stockholm, for example, 31 buses and 34 waste collection trucks operate on biogas (fuel made from clean-burning plants). In addition, the city operates 300 ethanol buses; it has, in fact, the largest clean vehicle fleet in the world. By 2020, the city expects that 100 percent of its transit fleet will be clean-air operant (Beatley 41).

Solar energy produces many beneficial contributions to our planet, but, as with everything in life, there are always cons that come along with the most fruitful benefits. The starting costs of installing solar panels are very high—a big investment many corporations are not willing to make. Although solar panels' productivity is not extensively dependent on the climate, the number of hours of sunlight available plays a huge factor on the wattage of power received. As a result, more panels would need to be installed in areas that may not receive enough sunlight. Furthermore, as Sheila Bocchine writes, "They also only work when the sun is shining. At night you will have to rely on stored energy from net metering or have an alternative system" (1). Nevertheless, solar power produces positive long-term results that will inevitably outweigh whatever factors may seem prohibitive.

> The author looks at both sides of the proposition to go solar.

It is important to be educated on the effects fossil fuels have on our planet; it is equally important to make strides in reversing these effects. Clearly, cities can be gateways to a cleaner planet if only we change the way we operate them. Thus, we all need to urge our urban leaders to go green before it is too late. We need to say no to the fossil fuels that are suffocating our planet in greenhouse gases and recognize that solar power is more than simply an alternative energy source. The sun may prove our only alternative if humankind is to have a future.

> The author's conclusion does more than simply summarize her essay; it makes a poignant call for action.

-------------------- Works Cited

Beatley, Timothy. "Envisioning Solar Cities:
    Urban Futures Powered By Sustainable Energy."
    Journal of Urban Technology 14:2 (2007): 31—
    47. Print.

Bocchine, Sheila. "Pros and Cons of Solar Power/
    Panels." *Earth 911.* 15 October 2007. Web. 7
    June 2008.

Brown, Eliot. "Bloomberg Wants Solar Panels on
    City Buildings." *The New York Observer* 8 April
    2008. Web. 7 June 2008.

City of New York. "PlaNYC 2030" 1 May 2008. Web. 8
    June 2008.

Revkin, Andrew C., and Matthew L. Wald. "The
    Energy Challenge: Solar Power Wins Enthusiasts
    but Not Money." *New York Times* 1 May 2006.
    Lexis-Nexis. New York City College of
    Technology Library, Brooklyn, NY. Web. 16 June
    2008.

Wald, Matthew L. "The Energy Challenge: Turning
    Glare into Watts." *New York Times* 6 March
    2008. EBSCO-Academic Premier. New York City
    College of Technology Library, Brooklyn, NY.
    Web. 1 June 2008.

Heading is centered.

List is alphabetized by author's last name (or by title when a work has no author). The first line of each entry is not indented; subsequent lines are.

Publication date appears first, followed by the date the author's accessed the article.

Double-spacing is used throughout.

If your website does not have an author, write the sponsoring organization (if there is neither an author nor a sponsoring organization, begin with the title of the website). Include date of publication or last revision, access date, and address of website.

Put last name first only for one author when an article is co-authored.

For entries from online library databases, name the database, library, location, and date of access.

© Analene Bumbury, NYCCT student, 2008

THE APA STYLE

The APA (American Psychological Association) style is used for courses in the social sciences, such as psychology, sociology, anthropology, and economics, and the life sciences. This style asks that you put the last name of the author and the year of publication in parentheses immediately after any research information. A list of sources entitled **References** also needs to appear at the end of your paper. Your **References** page provides full bibliographic information about the books, articles, and other documents you have used.

APA in-text citations

Citations are required for all print and electronic sources. These are examples of the most common.

Author's name in main sentence; year of publication in parentheses

A recent study by Michals (2008) demonstrated that after forty-five minutes, students tend to lose 80% of their cognitive attention.

Author's names and year in parentheses

One study suggests that in addition to verbal information, memory involves spatial and visual cues (Pastor, 2007).

More than one author cited in the same parentheses

Many current studies (Pastor, 2005; Crane, 2014; Horley, 2008) have suggested that ravens are capable of complex types of cognitive processing.

Several sources by the same author

Several studies by Horley (2009, 2012, 2015) have demonstrated that birds and humans share similar innate tendencies for ordering their environment.

Quotation

Jones (2003) acknowledges that "although the divorce rate is increasing, most young children still dream of getting married" (p. 34).

The author states that "more than fifty percent of all marriages end in divorce" (Jones, 2003, p. 145).

Unknown author

Global warming has led to the emergence of microbes that resist most antibacterial soaps ("Global Disaster" 2007).

No date

Forton (n.d.) expresses disapproval of the American welfare system.

APA Citations (for References page)
Books
Single Author:
Bryant, F.C. (2013). *Children from Beyond.* Cambridge: Boston College Press.

Two or More Authors:
Smiley, J. & Thompson, F. (2007). *Primates: a world of their own.* Jackson, MS: University Press of Mississippi.

Anonymous:
Dictionary of Large Scenes (3rd edition). (2010). New Haven: Goose Press.

Edited:
Franklin, J. P. (Ed.) (2005). *Case studies in psychology today.* New York: Oxford University Press.

Chapter in an Edited Book:
Menendez, M. (2005). Working with young children in China. In J.P. Franklin (Ed.) *Case studies in psychology today* (pp. 155–182). New York: Oxford University Press.

Articles in Newspapers and Periodicals
Newspaper:
Broden, J. (2008, February 26). Going green at CUNY. *New York Tech Times*, p. 16.

Broden, J. (2008, February 26). Going green at CUNY. *New York Tech Times*, p. 16. Retrieved June 20, 2008, from the LexisNexis Academic database.

Magazine:
Peters, J. (2006, November 14). Zoo animals in trouble. *New Yorker*, 45–47.

Peters, J. (2006, November 14). Zoo animals in trouble. *New Yorker*, 45–47. Retrieved December 20, 2006, from the Academic Search Premier database.

Scholarly Journal:

Dollaghan, Christine A. (1987). Fast mapping in normal and language-impaired children. *Journal of Speech & Hearing Disorders*, 52(3), 218–222.

Adilson,Daniel C. (2011). Reshaping New Minds. *Journal of Child Learning,* 16 (2), 206-222.

Film

Langston, C. (Producer) & Tossil , B. (Director). *Making Man Again* [Motion Picture]. United States: Virgin Pictures.

Interviews, email, and other personal communication:

Personal communication should not be listed in your reference list. Instead, parenthetically cite (intext citation only) providing communicator's name, the phrase "personal communication," and the date of the communication.

Example: (D. Galvin, Personal Communication, January 1, 2015).

CHICAGO MANUAL STYLE OF WRITING

The Chicago Style of writing, also referred to as Turabian, is yet another documentation style. The Chicago Manual style of writing can be used within the disciplines of literature, history, and the arts. It is, quite frankly, the "old school" of writing styles.

Like MLA and APA, it too has a distinct set of guidelines as they relate to documentation and format. Chicago style tends to focus more heavily on **endnotes (notes that are placed at the end of the essay/research paper)** and **footnotes (notes that appear at the bottom of the page)**, and it also has a very specific set of guidelines as they relate to the bibliography.

Just as the MLA and APA styles of writing have rules about titles, formatting, publication information, and punctuation, so too does the Chicago Style of writing. If you are asked to use this style of writing, do not take any chances. Chicago Style is very detailed and specific. We recommend that you visit the Purdue OWL website, read the current version of the Chicago Style Manual (chicagomanualofstyle.org), or read the most recent version of Kate L. Turabian's *Manual for Writers of Research Papers, Theses, and Dissertations.*

Constructing the Cover Page

Keep in mind, for major papers that represent a large percentage of an academic course or are a requirement for a degree, a title page is standard. All manual styles have examples of title pages.

Sample:

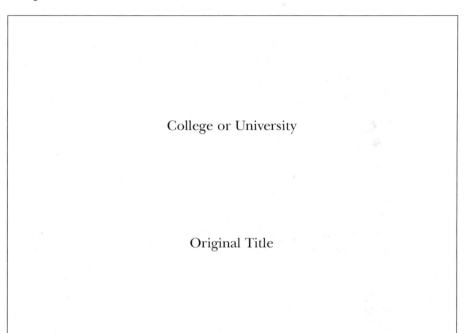

College or University

Original Title

Name

Course and number

Professor

Due date

Submitted in Partial Fulfillment of the Requirements for ...

Below is a listing of guidelines for the three dominant manual styles:

- MLA doesn't require a cover page.
- APA does require a cover page.
- Chicago style only requires a cover page if the writing is more than five pages long.
- APA requires a *running head* flush left with the page header (see apa.org or Purdue OWL for example).
- APA has an *Author Note* line, but only if required by the instructor.
- The title, author, class, professor, and date for Chicago Style is centered on the page and double spaced.
- When the page includes the name of college or university, it goes either at the top or bottom.
- The title appears about a third of the page down from the top.
- Farther down on the page should be the course, professor's name, and due date. For a thesis or dissertation, what the paper fulfills (Submitted in Partial Fulfillment...) with regard to the class or degree is standard (many seminar classes and papers that are a major portion of the grade may also require this line). **While all manual styles have the same basic requirements, see the latest update for the exact wording and format.**

final thoughts

As we are nearing the end of this endeavor, we would be remiss if we did not reiterate the following sentiment: Completing the writing assignment, research paper, or essay does NOT mean that you are done. Part of developing writing skills includes improving your skills as a reviser and an editor. In short, YOU MUST REVIEW YOUR WORK WHEN YOU ARE DONE WRITING. Moreover, if at all possible, please allow someone—an instructor, a respected peer, or tutor at a writing lab—to read your work before you submit the final assignment.

When editing or reviewing your work, both you and your reviewer should consider the following checklist:

The most common errors in writing.

Wrong word

Sentence fragment

Vague pronoun

Unnecessary comma

Missing or incomplete citation

Wrong or missing verb ending

Missing comma after an introductory element

Spelling

Incorrect quote usage (block quote or bracket error)

Missing signal phrase (before quote)

Missing word

Tense shift

Comma splice (use of comma to combine two distinct sentences)

Unnecessary or missing apostrophe

Run-on sentence

Awkward transition